CULTIVATING
culture

The official list of contributing authors is as follows (alphabetical by last name):

Dawn Cacciotti
Adam Calli
Teri Cirillo
Jen Hamilton
Michael Harper
Jill Heineck
Cindy Hines
Mark Leonardi
Nicole Price
Cheryl Schofield
Leslie S. Schreiber
Cynthia M. Schuler
Ken Silay
April L. Taylor

Book typeset by Kevin Williamson
Cover design by Kevin Williamson

Created in the United States of America

22 21 20 19 18 17 16   1 2 3 4 5

ISBN 978-0-9981714-5-6

Note from the Publishers

First, we want to acknowledge this esteemed collection of authors and extend a hearty thanks and congratulations to them. As with each anthology, Cathy and I—the curators, editors, and publishers—have the privilege to be first reading our contributors' wisdom, and it's always a special treat to work with their material in this way. We're consistently impressed by our authors, but each new anthology seems to raise the bar a bit higher. The authors of *Cultivating Culture* have, in their turn, put splendid work forward. We thank them for their diligence, insight, and professionalism working with us—and one another.

Accordingly, we would also like to thank our network of authors from Red Letter Publishing's Professional Series anthologies, including our most recent titles *Evolution of Human Resources* and *Lessons in Leadership*. It's a privilege to remain connected with this growing community as the Professional Series continues (and evolves) into 2017.

Many thanks also to Sharon Armstrong of the SAA Trainers and Consultants Network, a free referral service for HR, OD, trainers, coaches, and keynote speakers. Sharon is a HR consultant and author, and she was very helpful to us as we began to develop this anthology. She can be reached at (202) 333-0644 or online at www.trainersandconsultants.net.

The *culture* of an organization is an abstract, immaterial thing—yet culture is very real, and it's monumentally important for the health of a business, both in terms of the people's happiness and in terms of the bottom line. In this anthology, our authors offer their measured suggestions for how you can cultivate a healthy, forward-thinking culture in your organization; theirs is a comprehensive and robust set of recommendations.

Like any matter of value, a good culture requires time and investment—but it needn't be complex as rocket science. If the advice that follows is any indication, improving culture can be friendly—and even fun!

— *Cathy Fyock and Kevin Williamson*

A Brief Postscript—

If you would like to contribute to a professional anthology—We have our first 2017 entry in the Professional Series, *Humans at Work*, which will open for reservations in January 2017. Spots are filled on a first-come-first-served basis. *Humans at Work* is expected to release in June of 2017. Email cathy@cathyfyock.com to reserve your spot!

To ask any questions, propose topic suggestions, or inquire about custom projects, visit our website at RedLetterPublishing.com/Anthologies for FAQs and more information.

Red Letter Publishing and Cathy Fyock are proud to partner with the SHRM Foundation in presenting this Professional Series anthology.

100% of publisher proceeds from Amazon sales of this book will benefit the SHRM Foundation.

The SHRM Foundation is a values-based charity organization whose mission is to champion workforce and workplace transformation by providing research-based HR solutions for challenging inclusion issues facing current and potential employees, scholarships to educate and develop HR professionals to make change happen and opportunities for HR professionals to make a difference in their local communities. Some of the challenging inclusion issues the SHRM Foundation is taking on include: solving aging workforce issues; integrating veterans into the workforce; creating equal gender opportunities; ending employment discrimination; and integrating and engaging individuals with disabilities into the workforce.

The SHRM Foundation prepares HR professionals to take on these challenges by offering scholarships to return to school, participate in developmental seminars and conferences, and obtain SHRM professional certifications. Effective HR practice begins with the knowledge and competency to apply that knowledge. The SHRM Foundation is dedicated to making these educational opportunities open to all HR professionals and students, no matter what life challenges are facing them.

Finally, the SHRM Foundation supports the SHRM chapters and state councils by providing opportunities they can engage in locally to make a difference in their organization and community. Volunteer activities, chapter and programming ideas, fundraising events, and new member recruitment messages are among the resources the SHRM Foundation provides to these groups. All of these resources will focus on inspiring and empowering HR profession to lead transformation that will result in more inclusive organizations that provide opportunities for all types of employees to thrive.

The SHRM Foundation's vision is a world where empowered HR professionals build inclusive organizations where all employees thrive and organizations achieve success.

Contents

Dawn Cacciotti

Strong Corporate Cultures Aren't Accidents

Earlier this year, I got a phone call from a CEO I know. This CEO's company was crafting a platform that they hoped would help organizations build a strong corporate culture and engage their employees. Sure, the CEO had just pitched it to me as an employee engagement booster—but when he asked me what *my* clients were doing to engage their employees, I said it depended on their corporate culture. It would also depend upon where we stood along our plan to build and advance that corporate culture.

People often think that organizational cultures just *happen*. Sometimes, the people with that notion are companies who don't focus on organizational culture, or don't have an established plan for it. But people in a strong, positive, and lasting corporate culture know better: it's not an accident. Great cultures are created by design—and maintained by consistent work.

When I first meet with a new or potential client, often a CEO or a room of business leaders, one of the first questions I ask is for them to describe their organization's current culture. This question always seems to make them pause. I don't believe anyone's ever had an answer ready. That's not to say the leaders haven't thought about their culture, that they don't care about or wish to build a strong and lasting culture. Most times, after all, the leaders to whom I'm speaking have reached out for that very reason: they're looking to build a strong human-capital infrastructure that will support the culture they want to build. But the question shows that most leaders have not sit down to construct a strategy for building and maintaining this all-important area. Most aren't even sure where to begin.

When I work with organizations to help build a great culture, I believe it's important to start the quest with the organization's mission or vision. The mission and/or vision of the organization helps shape the organization's path. It serves as a guidepost—or at least it should.

I was conducting a session about a year ago for over 100 small business owners. I asked everyone in the room to raise their hand—and to keep their hands raised—if they had a written mission or vision statement for their company. All one hundred hands went up. Then, I asked the group: if I were to visit your place of business and start walking the halls, and I asked your team members what your mission statement was, how many of you think they could tell me? After most of the hands went down, I only saw three hands still raised. I asked the remaining three leaders if they thought their team members were truly passionate about the mission or vision of the organization. One hand was left raised.

The goal, for any company, is to have every hire and every team member passionate for the direction and vision of the company that they work with. If there is a lack of passion, it can be devastating to the company and its collective drive to build a great corporate culture. In most cases, a company's mission is written down, then never discussed or referred to again. It isn't remembered when leaders make strategic decisions, it isn't taken into account when hiring, and it certainly isn't considered in the day-to-day activities within most offices. Most mission statements I've seen are long, drawn out, jargon-laden, and ultimately meaningless. It is imperative that we not only continue to share the mission and vision of our organization, but *integrate* it in the minds of our people so that we can build upon the passion that drove them to us in the first place. Remember that, in part, someone's passion and personality are the reason we hired them; if we can harbor that passion, we can continually build upon it to advance innovation, retain our talent and competitive advantage, increase our productivity and well-being, and ultimately surpass our strategic goals.

What we are looking to provide our team members is a clear direction and path for everyone in the organization to follow. Whether your organization has a mission statement, a vision statement, or both, what we need to provide our team members are *answers* to pertinent questions that will expand on the mission and vision statements. These answers should explain *why* the organization is in business, what the core values of the organization are, how each person in the organization impacts overall success, and ultimately why any stakeholder (client, member, customer, shareholder, team member) should care about the organization's product or service. Providing these answers builds the foundation for an organization's culture. The answers to these questions help shape the human capital infrastructure that leaders are looking to create. Having the answers to these questions and sharing them with team members are critical to shaping the path and strategic direction of the organization. Having the answers to these questions also allows the team member to fully understand the organization's history, buy in to the current strategy and direction, become part of a team that is working together to achieve the organization's goals, and collectively share in the passion that is driving the company's success.

There is one question that I believe should be answered before the others, since I believe it shapes the answers to the questions after it. That first question is about your organization's **core values**. Core values showcase the ideal behaviors and deep beliefs of the organization. The core values should positively support the mission and vision of the organization.

Many organizations do not provide clarity around their values, and many are not in consensus over what the values should be. Part of the misunderstanding is that core values are not (and should not be) keywords on your website, a slogan on your letterhead, or speech fodder for times of crisis. The core values are much more important; they are another set of key standards that allow team members to know what the organization wants and expects—from them and for itself. Core values create accountability.

It's important to put a description behind the core values, to state more specifically what the core value looks like in a day-to-day setting. What often creates misunderstanding and conflict here is precisely *how* everyone is supposed to act, or what is acceptable behavior for achieving the values. This is an essential conversation: clarifying 'how' an organization will meet the standards set by their core values. This helps eliminate disruption and chaos throughout the day-to-day.

Since leaders of the organization determine, define, and describe the core values of the organization, including how they look on an average day, it's important that leaders have consensus about acceptable behavior and open routes to fulfilling company values. This may seem simple or trite, but it isn't—each of us has a different internal value system that guides us (often silently) in our actions. It's an error to assume everyone sees through our own personal lens, and it's the downfall of many leadership teams and organizations trying to build a strong culture. Leadership must be 100% clear on what the core values are, what they look like in the day-to-day activities of the organization, and how they are to be achieved. Last but not least, leadership must also be the role model of these values at all times if they expect the rest of the organization to follow them.

When developing a plan for building a strong organizational culture, it becomes clear immediately how important it is to communicate clearly and concisely. Every strategic initiative put into motion requires effective communication throughout, and it's no different with the creation and maintenance of a strong organizational culture. Culture demands effective communication at all levels, and through all means possible. There needs to be a continuous, healthy flow throughout the organization—and what determines the health of that continuous flow is the picture of the culture the organization is trying to create. Is your organization moving in the right direction?

I hear from a lot of organizations that they want an open-door atmosphere of communication. Well, what does that mean, exactly? How does that play out on a typical day? Can a team member drop in on the President of the organization any time they want—or will they need an appointment to meet with them? Is the company planning on physically redesigning their floor plan to have everyone in cubicles, without any separate offices, so communication can flow with no barriers? If there are offices, are people supposed to leave the doors open? If the door is closed, can people knock and enter? Are all-staff meetings conducted for "downloading" all information, or does information pass through department meetings run by the middle managers? These are just a few of the specific questions, and the answers to them play a big role in determining the culture of an organization. There is no right answer. It's just a matter of accomplishing what you set out to do for creating your organizational culture—and making sure that there is an established plan to reach that outcome.

I have run numerous engagement surveys for organizations, and communication always seems to be one of the lowest-rated areas in corporate culture efforts. For those of us in Human Resources, it's always an area where we shake our heads and wonder how we can do better, how can we communicate any more than we already have. I've discovered along the way to building strong organizational cultures that it wasn't always that leaders failed to share the information, or that there was a failing to use every vehicle known to man to get the messages out. In most instances, the problem stemmed from *how* we were getting this information out. We weren't making use of our most important vehicles for advancing the message about our culture. We weren't communicating *through* our people.

Making use of our own people as culture ambassadors was probably the single biggest breakthrough I have had helping organizations become employers of choice. When you're able to engage your teams in the decision-making of your culture—where and how it is being directed and built—they might surprise you by passionately jumping in and concocting some of the cleverest, most original, and funniest ways of accomplishing things—including many which you may not have thought of before.

Of course, there is a strategic way to use culture ambassadors. There is (and should be) a plan for it. Create specific key groups around culture topic areas, ask for volunteers to those groups, and ask for a year's commitment. Then, ask the group to select a leader (help build leadership skills), provide them with goals to accomplish (build accountability), give them a budget (teach resourcefulness and fiscal responsibility), and ask each group to report periodically (monthly or quarterly) to the organization on what they're doing and accomplishing (boost facilitation skills and so much more).

Culture ambassadors don't always need to belong to established groups. They can be individuals you seek out to help with communicating upcoming initiatives. These select individuals can be key advocates for getting communication out to other team members, and they might help to move the needle forward on getting buy-in for upcoming culture changes or other plans. Seek out key people in any and all levels of the organization; utilize them as champions, advocates, or mavens. Remember, it pays to ask for help, especially on the essential journey of improving communication throughout the organization.

There is certainly is a lot involved in making a great and lasting culture, and in this chapter we have discussed a number of topic areas that should give organizations a starting point. In parting, this is what I must stress to you: that it is beyond important to have a plan and strategy around the culture you are seeking to create. And not only do you need a plan of action, but you need clarity and consensus about that plan in order for it to help you reach your goal. As in every plan, there should be room for evaluation and measurement; if things aren't moving in the right direction, don't be afraid to say so and propose constructive changes. Get feedback from all; listen; be willing to try new things. Most of all: wherever you can, have fun with your people (or your team) along the way.

Happy planning!

ABOUT THE AUTHOR
Dawn Cacciotti
SPHR, HCS, SHRM-SCP

Dawn Cacciotti, founder of EngageHRnow® has over 25 years of strategic HR experience. As a Human Resources strategist, author, and passionate speaker, Dawn is an advocate for the importance of strategic HR to the success of all organizations.

EngageHRnow, founded in 2014, is a Human Resources consulting and outsourcing firm specializing in employee engagement, organizational culture, and human capital solutions for small to mid-size associations and for-profit business.

Dawn has won numerous honors for her leadership in the area of Engagement, Strategy and Well-being. In 2014 she was recognized by Employee Benefits News as the "Benefits Leadership – Judges Choice" award winner for her well-being program that focused on physical, financial and emotional well-being and led the strategic human capital change for a well-respected association—allowing them to be awarded a spot on the coveted *Washington Post* Top Workplace list in Washington, D.C.. Dawn was also a Human Resources Strategic Alignment honoree for the HRLA awards.

EngageHRnow's vision statement—*Get Them to Great*—exemplifies the passion that Dawn has for partnering with organizations that are not satisfied with just being good; they are ready to become great! Dawn is experienced at advising senior executives and staff on HR best practices and provides essential leadership throughout the implementation of strategic HR solutions. She assists organizations to effectively build their Human Resources infrastructure and guides the leadership team in developing the organizational culture while educating and engaging the staff on how they directly impact the overall success of the business.

Dawn currently resides in Alexandria, Virginia.

EMAIL dcacciotti@engagehrnow.com **WEBSITE** http://www.engagehrnow.com
PHONE 571-458-7890 **LINKEDIN** /in/dawncacciotti **FACEBOOK** /engagehrnow
TWITTER @dcacciotti

Adam Calli

Internal Mobility:
Embedded in Culture, Driven By Data

The cultural and organizational benefits of strong internal mobility programs are well-documented in current human capital literature. In this chapter, we'll explore how you can use data to drive internal mobility programs and monitor their results—then how you can integrate them into your operations. We'll also explore some questions that you might share with your leadership and HR teams to get them thinking as well.

> "If we are unable to hire or retain key employees or a highly skilled and diverse workforce, it could have a negative impact on our business. Our continued growth requires us to hire, retain and develop our leadership bench and a highly skilled workforce. We compete to hire new employees and then must train them and develop their skills and competencies. Failure to develop an adequate succession plan to backfill current leadership positions, including our Chief Executive Officer, or to hire and retain a diverse workforce could deplete our institutional knowledge base and erode our competitive advantage. In addition, our operating results could be adversely affected by increased costs due to increased competition for employees."

— *PepsiCo 2013 Annual Shareholder Report*

Even for PepsiCo—one of the largest and wealthiest companies in the world—talent attraction, retention, and development were important enough to mention in their annual shareholder's report. These issues are important enough to you that you're reading this book.

The cultural and business benefits of internal mobility can't be discussed if we don't know what internal mobility is! According to Bersin by Deloitte, "Internal Mobility (AKA mobility and talent mobility) is a dynamic internal process for moving talent from role to role at the leadership, professional, and operational levels."

The key elements of this definition are first that it's *dynamic*—in other words, it's an active and vibrant effort. Second, that it's a *process*—it happens in an organized and methodical way. Lastly, that it happens in multiple roles at multiple levels—so it is not limited in scope like many imagine!

As you continue reading this chapter, ask yourself this: What's the biggest obstacle to embracing talent mobility in my organization? Keep your answer in mind as you read on…

As we explore internal mobility and data, we'll be considering these topics from three points of view:

1. The Organization's
2. The Employee's
3. The Data's (yes, data can have a point of view!)

Before we begin with an organizational point of view, ask yourself this from the organization's perspective: What's the goal of our mobility program? Your goals for this program not only drive the dynamic process, but they ultimately impact how satisfied your employees will be with the opportunities you present to them as a result.

To get an idea of some goals, let's have a look at what organizations stand to gain from effective internal mobility programs:

> "Successful internal mobility programs help hiring managers learn about the skills, experiences and aspirations of internal candidates, while employees learn about new roles that will allow them to contribute to the organization in new and different ways. This kind of organizational transparency can increase employee engagement and retention while shortening time to productivity and reducing competitive intelligence leakage."
>
> — *David Marzo, Vice President and General Manager of Korn Ferry subsidiary Futurestep, November 2015 while discussing the results of a recent executive survey.*

Compare the results of this survey against the definition of *culture* provided by Deloitte in their 2016 Global Human Capital Trends report. There, culture is defined as "the way things work around here," and engagement as "how people feel about the way things work around here." The point here is that providing staff an opportunity to move throughout your organization does more than just provide career growth for the person moving. It also provides an opportunity to reinforce your culture and demonstrate your values by committing to your team in certain ways.

Meanwhile, if *engagement* is (as Deloitte indicates) "how people feel about the way things work around here," then surely employees would feel good having the chance to pursue new challenges and see colleagues doing the same.

As you assess the value of an internal mobility program for you, and consider ways to encourage its initiation, think about the needs of a few different employee populations:

- The C-Suite and senior management
- Mid-level managers
- Millennials and other generational groups

What's the best way to discover their needs, you wonder? Ask them! This information-gathering phase can be critical to the long-term success of the program! Ask people what they want to know. Ask what the best way is for them to get the info. Then, as you construct your reasoning for the establishment (or continuation) of an internal mobility program, you'll be doing so with the wants and needs of other major constituencies in mind. The feedback they give will guide your system selection, staff involvement, and communications efforts around data and mobility.

As you prepare to approach your leaders and peers to discuss talent mobility, ask yourself these questions as well:

- Has your organization traditionally embraced talent mobility?
    — If not, why not? What were/are the barriers?
    — Have any business drivers changed? For example, if you're now in growth mode, you have different talent needs compared to a company holding steady!

- If your organization has embraced talent mobility...
    — What are managers and employees accustomed to seeing and doing?
    — What should you consider starting to do, perhaps to improve the program, and what shouldn't be changed that's working well?

- How is the expectation of talent mobility reflected in your performance management system?
    — How do you track if employees are ready to transfer or promote?
    — As an example, a company I worked for used a three-category scale for its managers to gauge their readiness for promotion:

    (A) Well-placed
    (B) Promotable 0-6 months
    (C) Promotable 7-12 months

- If beneficial, during the performance appraisal cycle, your organization should ask about and track things like:

    (A) Employee willingness to relocate and to where
    (B) Jobs and departments they're interested in

While we're discussing performance management, let's discuss its cousin: reward and recognition. Organizations often track what prior positions an employee has held, but . . . do you track who their prior managers were? Consider how valuable it would be to know which members of your management team are your best "farmers" of talent! Much like farmers celebrate harvesting a good crop, organizations should celebrate managers who are proven mentors for growing new talent.

Ask yourself this: What's the value, to my organization, of a manager who has successfully promoted numerous employees who have not only become successful in their own right, but who've also mentored and developed others along the way?

Then ask: How do we appropriately reward those managers who are successfully growing the next generation's leaders? Think about these questions, and you might see already how integrating talent development into your performance management efforts, and then rewarding it, is a sure way to construct a strong and magnetic corporate culture!

From performance management, we move now to your managers' job descriptions (JDs) and ask another question: What do your JDs say about the managers' duty to train, mentor, and promote talent?

Regardless of a manager's department or specialty, managers of people face many common challenges and have many common responsibilities. Are those all articulated clearly in the JD? Is anything said of their role in talent development, or is it solely focused on the daily tasks and responsibilities which the manager is expected to perform? If the JD and performance appraisal are both silent on that matter, if no rewards or recognition are focused on talent development efforts, then ask yourself this question: How much WILL our managers try to develop our talent?

Another cultural benefit of performance management and rewards systems that encourage talent promotion is that they help to eliminate the cultural stagnation caused by "talent hoarders." Can you—on a consistent, organization-wide basis—answer who "owns" talent? Of course, individuals own their own talent, and will take it where they like—but from the firm's point of view, the "owner" of talent should be the organization, not the manager!

Managers who are "talent hoarders" are the ones who seek to keep the best talent in their department, who stymie staff promotions and transfers for their own selfish good. Clearly, they are not looking out for the organization's best interests. Culturally speaking, their actions demotivate the staff, erode the cultural foundation, and undermine organizational engagement efforts. Allowing them to continue to hoard talent is tacit approval of their actions—and in a sense, the surrender of your culture to those who care for it least. Tracking data on manager transfer and promotion history allows you to identify and eliminate those bottlenecks.

And make no mistake, bottlenecks do exist! Consider this revelation from the November 2015 Korn Ferry Futurestep survey: that "nearly one-third of executives surveyed said employees have to keep their intent to apply for new positions within their [own] company a secret from their current managers." In other words: employees feel a need to hide from their own boss that they want to make moves somewhere else in the same company. If this is where you are, you're bottlenecked.

Once bottlenecks are removed, you need some methods to foster mobility—actually making it possible for employees to transition as they are intended to. One method common in unionized workplaces, job bidding, is a smart practice with a strong data component. In job bidding, employees formally indicate their interest in a position they feel qualified for, but before that position becomes available. HR reviews employment history, training, and other qualifications to determine if the person is qualified. This way, they can be considered automatically when such a position opens. If the person is not deemed qualified at the time they submit the bid, the employee can work on enhancing their skills to begin preparing themselves now for those future opportunities. It'd be fairly easy to ask an employee if there are roles in the company they'd want to bid for—so consider integrating that into your performance management process.

There are secondary motives and indirect reasoning for internal mobility programs. According to *The 2020 Workplace - How Innovative Companies Attract, Develop, and Keep Tomorrow's Employees Today*, "The US Department of Labor predicts that US-based employers will need 30 million new college-educated workers in the next decade, while only 23 million young adults are expected to graduate from college during that period." This means our workforce will most likely have a seven-million-employee short-fall soon—meaning talent will be scarce. It stands to reason that an organization which does a better job attracting and keeping talent will be in a much stronger competitive position. Effective internal mobility programs help create a culture that allows you to compete more effectively, especially at keeping your own talent.

Previously, I mentioned asking different groups what they'd want out of a talent mobility program. One specific way to do this is to ask employees what they would like their next job to be like.

In the "Generations at Work" survey also conducted for *The 2020 Workplace*, respondents were given a choice of 15 characteristics they'd want most for their next job. The number one characteristic both Millennials and Gen Xers will seek out when choosing their next job is that it "will develop my skills for the future." But if you offer them ways to develop their talents—if you offer them their next job, and on the heels of helping them professionally, they might not need (or ever want) to leave—which, again, places your organization in prime position.

Here's yet another reason to embrace talent mobility. According to the February 9, 2016 Wall Street Journal—referencing the Department of Labor's monthly Job Openings and Labor Turnover Survey (JOLTS) report—voluntary quitting has hit its highest level in nine years. It is returning to pre-recession levels! This means that your employees not only *can* leave, but *are leaving.* Once again, your internal mobility programs can be an effective tool to make them want to stay, despite the increasing temptation to leave that they might otherwise have.

I mentioned at the beginning that data has a point of view—and as I've suggested throughout, it's important to collect and maintain data wherever possible. But no discussion of data would be complete without considering that data's quality. To wit—there's an expression that's been around about as long as there have been computers: GIGO, or Garbage In Garbage Out.

At the most basic level, Garbage In Garbage Out just means that computers can never produce perfect results if the people using them don't provide the right inputs (or program the computer correctly). It also suggests that, like a game of Telephone, data is subject to error and distortion each time it "changes hands," especially if a person passes the information manually. Finally, Garbage In Garbage Out offers the following stern caution: when people rely on you as a source of data, and they use that data to take action that has real impact in peoples' lives, you'd better get it right! Data can come from many sources; ensure the accuracy and completeness of the data you use from any of them.

Employee engagement surveys can be another great data source for insight into what employees think about their opportunities for career advancement—and in turn, what managers think about their ability to promote worthy staff members.

A quick check for you: Do you have questions on your employee engagement survey that address this topic?

Earlier, I said you should ask your leaders what they want to know when you're gathering information. There are a handful of things most leaders want to know about talent mobility, so at a minimum, come prepared with the following:

- How many internal people are applying for your openings?
- Who is applying?
- How do their qualifications match your needs?
- Why aren't more people applying?

If the promotable population is sparse and few people pursue internal opportunities, it could indicate you have a cultural problem.

Engagement and talent mobility have an opposite—turnover—which also bears a closer look when talking about moving talent to the right places. For instance, one often-overlooked data category is desirable turnover. In his April 2009 article "Not All Employee Turnover Is Bad — Celebrate Losing the Losers," Dr. John Sullivan writes that "at least 25% of all turnover is 'desirable' turnover." He provided 14 categories of departures where an employee leaving is not a bad thing!

Suppose, as one example, a sub-par performer voluntarily resigns or is terminated. Either way, it's turnover. One reason it's desirable turnover is obvious—a low performer dilutes the productivity and culture by staying. But it's desirable turnover for another reason: they're holding a position to which someone else might aspire and excel.

Track desirable turnover and you'll see progress being made towards the culture you want—and need for a competitive edge in the new millennium's fast-paced global economy. Sullivan's article is worth finding for your further reading!

If we discuss desirable turnover, we must discuss its counterpart, regrettable turnover. As with desirable turnover, there are many reasons why an employee's departure might be called regrettable. Imagine, for example, that a strong employee goes to a direct competitor. The fact that the person had been a strong contributor would make you sad enough to see them leave, but when they go to a competitor? THAT stings. Or how about the person who heads up R&D—or a salesperson who consistently exceeds quota? Those, too, are regrettable losses. If you have any kind of "high-potential" designation for next-generation leaders, you should certainly classify anyone so designated as a regrettable loss. There are multiple reasons why an employee's departure could be regrettable, but from a cultural point of view, what you should remember is that anyone who'd be regrettable to lose would probably also leave and take part of the culture with them!

A more positive metric that's designed to track internal mobility is the **Career Path Ratio.** This ratio reflects the number of employees moving upward in the organization as a percentage of all employee movement. It's an indicator of the career development opportunities that exist within your organization, and is calculated as follows:

$$\frac{\text{TOTAL PROMOTIONS [TP]}}{(\text{TOTAL PROMOTIONS [TP]} + \text{TOTAL TRANSFERS [TT]})}$$

$$\downarrow$$

$$\text{XX.xx\%}$$

For example: if in a given time period there were 100 total promotions (TP) and 40 transfers (TT), there would be a career path ratio of 71.42%.

To get the calculation correct, it's important to understand its elements, so when counting promotions, only include employees who moved to a higher-level position or one with greater responsibility. Lateral moves are transfers in which employees move to different departments or job categories, but with equal responsibility. While laterals play an important role in career growth and may position an employee for future advancement, they're not counted as promotions for this calculation. Look to your org charts, job descriptions, and exempt/non-exempt factors to be certain these are "coded" properly.

Going back to our definition of internal mobility, it's a "dynamic internal process for moving talent from role to role at the leadership, professional, and operational levels." Results like this sample (71.42%) would indicate you're dynamic, are actively moving staff, and have a formal process that managers support. Employees are probably rewarded for contributing, too, and it might also indicate employees who don't have to apply for internal openings in secret. Whatever your result, this metric can be tracked over time, by location, and even by manager.

As you can see, data is the enabling tool that can allow you to make better, faster talent management decisions. And like any of the best management decisions, talent development and mobility ultimately make strong positive contributions—not only to the bottom line, but to the culture that lives and breathes its work every day.

ABOUT THE AUTHOR
Adam Calli
SHRM-SCP, SPHR, SWP

Adam has over 18 years of comprehensive experience in all aspects of progressive human resource management, in such diverse environments as government contracting, television production, commercial banking, hospitality, and multi-client outsourced HR support. After graduating with his Bachelor's Degree from Florida State University, Adam began his career in hospitality industry operations before making the transition into HR.

He is now the Principal Consultant for Arc Human Capital, LLC where he provides support for organizations seeking to fulfill their compliance mandates while striving to constantly improve their human capital capabilities. He's also an HR instructor for George Mason University's Learning Solutions Division and Northern Virginia Community College's Workforce Development Division.

Adam has managed employees in many functions and has experience supporting blue and white collar organizations in privately held and publicly traded companies with multi-site operations. Adam has been quoted in HR Magazine, has presented for multiple SHRM Chapters, has delivered webcasts and podcasts for the Human Capital Institute, and has been a panelist for the American Society of Association Executives (ASAE) and the Northern Virginia Family Services (NVFS) Training Futures program. He is finishing his Masters in Management with an HR concentration at Catholic University, is a veteran of the US Navy Reserves, and holds his SHRM-SCP, SPHR, and SWP certifications.

Arc Human Capital is online at archumancapital.com. Adam is on Twitter @HRNole1 and is available via email at adam@archumancapital.com.

Adam dedicates his chapter to his kids C, J, & W:
You guys make me incredibly proud! I love you and am happy I'm your dad!

Teri Cirillo

The Art and Science of Cultivating a Great Culture

As I was traveling north through the beautiful Napa Valley on the way to my first consulting gig, I could smell the wine fermenting in the cellars along the way, and it reminded me how special and unique it is to live and work in wine country. This is God's country, as many like to say, and certainly one of my very favorite places in the world. It's a special place with special people.

One of the most unique things about the wine business is that it creates one of the very few products where you can control and directly influence the consumer's experience with the product—and all the way from the beginning to the end of the process, from earth to bottle to your palate.

To give you a sense of a wine tour experience in a paragraph: you can tour the vineyards and taste the wine grapes right off the vines. You can follow the grapes to the sorting table, to the crusher, destemmer and press, and see and smell the wine fermenting in the barrels or tanks in the cellar. You can even taste the wine directly from the barrel or tank during the fermentation process. Then you can follow the wine to the bottling line and see the labels being placed on the bottle either by hand or automatically. Then, of course, the most fun is tasting the finished wine from the bottle at the tasting room with a host who describes the story, aromas and flavors of the wines.

The wine industry is one of the few industries where you can experience the full process from earth to table—and also directly experience the culture of the people who make and cherish its product.

The art and science of building a great culture is similar to the art and science of creating great fine wine.

How do you make a small fortune in the wine business? Start with a large one! The wine industry is not for the faint of heart. You have to be in it for the long-term and ready to weather many storms—literally. Mother Nature will try to impact your destiny in the wine business, so you have to adapt for her. Cultivating a great culture is similar to creating a fine wine in that both take time, TLC, persistence, resilience, adaptation, and vision.

As Stephen Covey recommends, begin with the end in mind. In the wine industry, it starts with the terroir (the land and climate) and the rootstock, and you need foresight about supply and demand since it takes at least three years for the vines to mature enough to deliver enough quality fruit for great wine.

Whether you're in a start-up, turnaround, or continuous improvement operation, the leaders need to make a conscious choice about the desired culture. Every organization, group, or team has a culture whether you prescribe it or not. It may not become the culture you want if the leaders don't take an active role in developing and nurturing the culture on an ongoing basis. Even if you invented something brand-new, it's only a matter of time before your competitors will have the same knowledge, equipment, tools, and resources to compete on the product or service you are delivering. Eventually, therefore, the only guaranteed point of differentiation will be your people and culture.

I've been an HR Leader in start-ups, turnarounds, high-performing organizations, mergers & acquisitions, and divestitures for over twenty years—and the common denominators for success were always great leadership and culture.

Culture Defined

There are many definitions of culture. After discussions with several executive leaders in the industry, some of the common themes included the DNA of the company, the heart and soul of the company, the company's personality, how the work gets done, the common attitudes, beliefs and behaviors of the people within the company or organization, how people interact with one another, and the unspoken norms of the team.

My friends at The Rise Group describe culture as the collective attitudes and beliefs of the people. They define culture within the Attitude Model, whose four parts are (1) Experience, (2) Behavior, (3) Emotion and (4) Belief. Think of these as the quarters of a complete circle. Each of these four dimensions impact each other, and the sum of interpersonal experiences and interactions within the organization creates the culture. The leaders have the most powerful impact on the culture; how they respond to crisis or conflict, how they celebrate, and how they make decisions all have a daily influence over the culture. Being a leader in any type of organization is like living in a fishbowl: every move you make is visible, and people are watching.

It's important for each leadership group at the top to be able to define the culture for your organization, then to be able to articulate it and share it with others so that everyone has a shared definition and common language. Every organization needs to define its values and ask the question, what is the foundation that you are building on? Remember that values are different from behaviors and competencies.

Challenge yourself by asking the following questions:
- Who are you?
- Why do you exist?
- What do you stand for?
- What do you want to be known for?

Values shouldn't change—but the desired behaviors, competencies, and culture may evolve with the needs of the business as long as they are still aligned with the business's values. Values should also dutifully inform the mission and vision, again serving as a strong foundation made of rock, not sand.

Values are only worthwhile if they are lived. In the end, everyone should live the values—but more than anyone, especially at first, leaders need to live and breathe the culture for people to believe in it and follow them. Whatever the leaders do—or do not do—sends a message to the employees.

Culture in the Wine Industry

I've been an HR Leader in the Wine and Spirits Industry for over 15 years and worked with senior leaders from around the world. A common theme of motivators and values I discovered (as I was providing coaching for leadership development based on the Hogan assessment) is Hedonism. Keep in mind, this is not hedonism in the negative sense, but in the more literal sense: being motivated by variety and fun and entertaining others.

That seems fitting for the wine industry if you think about it. People in the wine industry aren't building rockets or software or curing cancer—but we're enhancing the lives of people who do those more serious things. Don't get me wrong: we take ourselves very seriously in the wine industry and believe in high-quality products and experiences. But it truly is more of a lifestyle choice and unapologetic passion for wine that draws us to the industry. According to The Hogan Guide, a high Hedonism culture is made of a lot of people who tend to "work hard and play hard" and believe that having fun and enjoying what you do should be as important to work as getting results. This is definitely true of most wine cultures.

Different cultures appeal to different people—just like wine. Some people may thrive in a certain culture where others may not. For a great fit, personal values should have some overlap with the company's or organization's values. People need to feel a sense of purpose and belonging, to be part of something bigger than themselves—to belong to a whole greater than the sum of its parts.

Whether you want a great sustainable culture or a great sustainable wine, you need to be in it for the long term. Identify how your purpose connects people and their work. Visualize what you want your culture to be and start to socialize it—start to speak and act like that picture in your head. Be honest with yourself and everyone around you, and take responsibility for the culture you belong to.

According to Jen Locke, a senior executive leader in the wine industry, "the front line is the bottom line." The tasting experience with the wine's host matters—and it can significantly impact the winery's bottom line. Cultivating a great culture therefore isn't just a matter of taste; a great culture creates real value for its business or organization.

Common themes of great cultures include:

1. Great leadership with forward-thinking vision—leadership from the top and in the middle drives great culture.
2. Consistent, honest, ongoing communication and feedback (through many forums and potentially in many languages).
3. Consistent sense that people are part of something bigger and contributing to a commonly-known purpose. There is a sense of community.
4. People know and value the culture so well that they hold each other accountable to living and sustaining it – from the day they're hired to the day they retire. Everyone takes responsibility for, talks about, and gives attention to the culture on a regular basis (especially leadership).

5. The culture adapts with the business in the most positive ways, always holding onto the values and what makes it special. Leaders foster, nurture, and guide the culture with the business changes.

Achieving fruition:

1. **Define your values.** Not just how you want people to behave; really dig deep to describe what you believe in. What's your foundation as a group? What do you always come back to? Talk is cheap; you can't build a foundation with sand.
2. **Walk the talk.** Your decisions and actions need to be aligned with those values. Do what you say and say what you mean.
3. **Engage and empower people (but actually).** Allow people to have autonomy and make decisions. Don't let any leaders treat people like children (and definitely don't do so yourself).
4. **Foster continuous improvement and growth** for both the people and products of your company.
5. **Be a benevolent employer.** Give employees the benefit of the doubt whenever possible. Treat all people with respect and dignity.
6. **Pay constant attention to the culture as you grow.** Viticulture and winemaking teams give the vines and wines constant attention throughout the winemaking process. They know the kind of quality they are seeking and adapt to Mother Nature's challenges along the way—what makes every vintage unique.
7. **Adapt to challenges with your foundation in mind.** Just as every year brings new challenges to the vineyards and winemaking process, the business environment will always bring new challenges to every organization's culture. You need to be prepared with a plan, have the end game in mind always, and adapt within the parameters of your foundation: values, vision, and mission.

To wrap it all up, here are the stages of cultural growth—as illustrated in concrete terms by the winemaking process (in brief) from grape to gullet.

Setting the Foundation (Vision and Strategy)
Planning the vineyard and planting the roots. Are you planting Pinot Noir or Cabernet? How many years will the vines need to mature? What long-term processes and decisions do you need to make?

Growth and Nurturing

Watering the grounds and tending the soil. Is every vine getting the right amount of water, even in drought conditions or strong sunlight?

Removal of Negative Elements

Pruning the vines, focusing on helping the ones who are contributing and developing with the most promise, making sure there's air and space for all the vines to grow, and removing the non-contributing or blighted vines who can prove toxic to healthy vines.

Continued Development and Planning

Preparing the vines and equipment to pick and process the grapes. Harvest season; completing processes, producing and finishing the product (including bottling), promoting the product or team and its successes, and preparing for next steps both with the products and the coming year's team.

Celebration and Return to Value

Taste the wine; that's your work, your blood and sweat and tears, everything you've worked for and worried about. This product stands for every reason you make wine. How does it taste—and what story do you want to tell others who taste it?

Addendum: Advice on Culture for Mergers & Acquisitions

According to The Rise Group, "Cultures should be respected, not revered."

Take, for example, one occasion where a special wine brand was acquired. The brand was unique, and the acquiring company was afraid to damage the brand by changing too much—so rather than go in and assess the situation as it stood, the acquiring company let the founder do what he wanted, but now with the acquiring corporation's money. Without much oversight, the situation quickly turned into a disaster.

There was an assumption that, since the brand had such a great reputation, the culture of the brand's employees was also great and shouldn't be disturbed. It turns out that was an (extremely) faulty assumption. The acquired company's leader ran, essentially, a dictatorship; he even had a button under his desk to order service, and he treated the company's employees like his personal servants. As a result, the working culture was horrible, toxic, and destructive. The leadership was full of tyrants, and without many advocates, the employees were being mistreated. Employees weren't allowed new gloves or sharp tools; the vineyard manager controlled their every move through coercion and manipulation. In fact, it wasn't until there was a threat from the United Farmworkers Union that the acquiring company became aware and got involved in the situation to begin changing the leadership.

Luckily, the winemaker himself was one of the kindest and most humble people I've ever met, and he helped establish the right culture along with new leadership—a culture that was aligned with the acquiring company's values. About a year later, after a lot of work, the workers' union was voted out and decertified—which is really unusual, but it happened because the employees realized they didn't need a union given the acquiring company's values and respect for them and their work.

To me, this reinforced the need to make leadership changes early to set the right expectations for developing a great culture in the next acquisition.

The next example is the family of a legacy tequila brand who decided it wanted to sell the company, but continue the legacy. They hired a "professional" who had previous experience with corporations to help prepare them to sell the company. As part of the acquiring company's leadership, we assessed their brand's leadership, and it became clear that the top leader had created a command-and-control environment; if he stayed, some of the top leaders who truly understood the people and business would leave.

We made the recommendation to the executive leadership team of the acquiring company that the top leader needed to leave and that we should bring someone from inside the acquiring company to lead and integrate the culture. The CEO and executive board members seemed shocked and surprised, but after much discussion, we convinced them it was the right thing to do. This made a tremendous difference right away; in fact, at the meeting when we communicated the leadership changes to the employees at the beginning of the process, they actually cheered and followed up to thank us each personally for making those changes. They were suddenly excited about the new leadership and culture, whose values were more aligned to the original family's values and culture.

When it comes to acquisitions and culture, leaders need to make a conscious decision. Which culture do you want to maintain and foster? Or should it be a merged version? How do the people in the acquired company feel about the changes? People expect change in the beginning, so make decisions, communicate, and be transparent. Don't manipulate or hide things from employees—that causes significant harm and mistrust. The leaders from the most successful mergers and acquisitions learn from both companies, and take the best elements from both to create an even better "new way." This can provide a significant competitive advantage and create an inclusive environment where everyone feels valued.

A special thanks goes to many of my friends and colleagues from the Wine Industry who shared their insights to help make this chapter come to life: Lisa Steiner, The Rise Group, Jen Locke, Steve Dorfman, Cheryl Nelson and Chris Fehrnstrom.

Teri Cirillo

MLHR

Teri Cirillo is an independent consultant and thought leader in HR consulting and leadership development. Teri has worked as a Human Resources leader for more than 20 years helping transform people and organizations to discover their gifts and reach their full potential.

Teri has broad business experience ranging from startups to business transformations to M&As and divestitures. She is therefore a business-focused, insightful Global Human Resource Executive who creates and implements strategies that drive business performance and international growth. Teri excels at aligning people, processes, and business strategy to increase engagement and productivity while reducing costs and risks. She is a proactive change agent who has successfully transformed corporate cultures, and she is a recognized expert in talent assessment, executive coaching, and leadership development.

Teri became a certified Senior Professional in Human Resources (SPHR) in 2002. She is a member of SHRM and is a certified coach in Neurocoaching and the Goldsmith Stakeholder Centered Coaching process. Teri holds a B.S. in Psychology from Northern Michigan University and a Master of Human Resources and Labor Relations from Michigan State University.

Teri is highly involved with the communities in which she lives, including membership in Leadership Mendocino (in California) and Leadership Louisville (while in Kentucky). She also volunteers for nonprofits' boards and various philanthropic organizations, such as Junior Achievement, Habitat for Humanity, and the Napa Valley Film Festival.

Teri has been married for 22 years and she has three children (and one dog). She spends her free time with her boys and in the great outdoors.

EMAIL teri.cirillo@gmail.com

PHONE 707-272-0109

Jen Hamilton

If You Can't Beat Them, Join Them

From Zero to Hero

Jan was fresh out of college—bright-eyed and full of accounting knowledge. She was lucky enough to land her dream job, a job working for one of the big, prestigious accounting firms. It was the kind of company that every accounting student dreamed of. In a chapter I'll skip, Jan would soon find that her dream would actually become a nightmare.

Jan had to do something else. She had a generous heart, so she chose to work with non-profits and higher-education clients. Her grand plan was to save these organizations from messing up their business practices so that they could do more good in the world. After all, she had an accounting degree; she knew what her clients needed to fix and wasn't afraid to tell them. As you can imagine, her delivery stunk with her know-it-all, entitled attitude. Unsurprisingly, she wasn't well-received. Her intentions had been good—but her approach had to change before she would lose her clients and then her job.

Jan didn't like not being liked. She decided to do something about it. First, she looked at her company for support. Even though her company had top-notch technical training, they didn't teach her how to be a bona fide professional or an excellent employee and they didn't teach her how to be great with the clients. Jan took matters into her own hands. She invested her own money and time outside of her busy work week attending professional development courses and reading books.

A funny thing happened. After Jan learned how to communicate, how to be respectful and responsible and accountable, Jan did get what she wanted. Jan got the chance to make a real difference improving her clients' businesses. She enhanced the work culture of her team at her firm by acting as a role model for other professionals. Then, people *did* like her. Jan went from Company Culture Zero to Hero.

I know Jan only too well. I am Jan. This describes me 20-plus years ago, in my career before I transitioned into corporate training. While I am not proud of my former arrogance, I am grateful for the lessons I learned during that time and that now I use to train companies. My investment into my professional development was the beginning of my commitment to be a catalyst for the kind of work cultures where the team is proud to be a part of the company, where they're excited to get to work in the morning. Whether in my former places of employment or the office of a client I serve, I train and empower everyone from frontline employees to senior management how to cultivate a culture of respect, honor each other, and engage one another meaningfully. Above all else, I learned that you don't need corner-office power to make your company a great place to work; you just need to care enough to take action.

Why have employees influence culture if they don't sit in the corner office?

It takes a village to raise a culture. Even a handful of the most engaging leaders isn't enough. You need a unified group to change an organization. When a leader sets the stage for launching a new initiative or improving the culture in some way, the next step is to empower and engage the employees who are not sitting in the executive suites. Initiatives tank if the people on the frontlines and in the middle don't adopt them and adapt to new ways.

Imagine a global company is rolling out a massive new software system. Once they roll it out, all of its facilities across the world will be using that one system. Overall, the concept makes a lot of sense: have employees share best practices and make the approach to certain matters consistent throughout the company. In theory, the idea would have wonderful potential for increased productivity and collaboration. However, from an employee point of view, the idea—in a word—stinks. Employees saw the new system as more hindrance than help.

When this company had tried something like this in the past, many people resisted it and ignored the new ways so they could keep working the same way they'd been used to. Sure, most employees tried the new way, but they'd slowly slip back into the old ways until, eventually, it was again as they'd always done it. The new system failed to stick, even when it was a good idea. With this latest attempt to roll out new software and systems, the company understood the risk of failure—the employees refuse to implement again—and decided to take a new approach.

I was hired to work with 100 of this company's employees, who were responsible for training their co-workers on this new software system. I was told that my task was to train them on how to effectively present this new system. But once I actually started working with this company, I realized the more important focus was to train these folks how to cultivate a culture of acceptance, and thereby nip the natural resistance to change in the bud. Leadership knew they would be unable to create buy-in to the new way without my guidance of frontline employees and management delivering the message of acceptance of this new initiative. When the whole village (and not just the town mayor) creates the culture of acceptance, initiatives become sticky and they last.

Whether it is acceptance of a new technology, a new product or service, or a new attitude you want from your employees, it will stick if the group changes the culture, not just because the big bosses said so. Let's face it: each of us human beings likes our own ideas a little better than ideas from people who exert power over us. Maybe there is a bit of teenage rebellion in all of us, but we like things our way. If employees don't have a say, they aren't likely to do cartwheels at any of the leaders' latest and greatest ideas, whether to improve culture or just about anything else in the company. If non-executive employees are not part of cultivating the culture, the new culture isn't likely to grow much—or at all.

How can I turn on the lights to see if they won't let me touch the light switch?

If you are an executive looking for ways to empower your team to cultivate culture—or if you are in a company where you would like to see an improvement in your work environment—here are three key strategies that have worked for my clients and my career:

- Role-model honoring and respecting others
- Manage-up and advocate for themselves
- Take responsibility for both what is working and what isn't working

Role-Model — Honor and Respect

Like moms would say, treat others how you want to be treated. When we first show honor and respect to others, we are more likely to receive the respect back. Being a role model for your teammates means they will start to follow your example of honoring and respecting.

Honoring means to see the best in people. In that light, give them the benefit of the doubt. Give thorough consideration to others' requests. For example: a co-worker says "I sent that email, didn't you get it?" and you swear you never got the email, then you later hear an apology from that co-worker because she found the email in her draft folder and forgot to send it to you. To honor her, resist being righteous. Say, "You are always so on top of it with emails, so don't worry about it. These things happen." By sharing that her normal way of communicating is timely, you honor that co-worker by focusing on her great attributes, and not the mistake.

Respect means to treat a person like they're a person. Be considerate and kind. Avoid damaging judgments, words, and actions. Listen and acknowledge that you heard and understood others, even if you don't agree or approve. A culture of respect in the workplace can sometimes look as simple as listening to people without interrupting, giving other people opportunities to voice their opinions, and adapting to others' needs and wants when you can.

Manage-Up and Advocate for Yourself

Being a catalyst for positive culture means working well with people at every level of the company. To be effective, team members need to engage their supervisors in a productive work relationship.

Manage-Up is a strategy to improve the working relationships, productivity, and results between team members and their supervisors. It works as an accountability tactic to ensure supervisors are meeting the expectations set by the company and their team members.

The Manage-Up strategy focuses on team members (A) communicating expectations with supervisors, (B) holding them accountable, and (C) advocating for yourself. The Manage-Up strategy is:

1. Take responsibility for effective communication by examining an issue from the supervisor's point of view. When sharing concerns or issues, acknowledge the supervisor's point of view first and then share a personal point of view.
2. Hold the supervisor accountable with kindness. If a supervisor's lack of follow-through impacts team members, explain how those actions affect the project and offer support to complete the task. State a goal for the overall work and the task, such as to be the best for the company.
3. Discuss the supervisor's preferred work style and address issues accordingly. For example, if a supervisor prefers email, use email before calling on the phone. Be adaptable and flexible. Encourage the entire team to support the supervisor and each other by acknowledging people's results and allowing for differences in approach.
4. Advocate for yourself and your ideas. To influence your working environment, at times you may need to speak up and request what you want instead of waiting for things to change or to be asked of you directly. For employees to successfully advocate for themselves, consider the following approaches:

A couple of tips:
- **Be confident, not cocky.** Confidence is knowing you will do your best. Cocky is knowing you are the best. When you know you will do your best, confidence shows up as a strong work ethic and makes people listen when you make requests. Being confident gives you the ability to recognize others for their great work because it is easier to see when others are doing their best, and you know you needn't feel threatened by their greatness.
- **Focus on commitment.** People focus on what they care about (their commitments and goals). When you look for what others care about, you can then find a way to align your goals and theirs. Then, make a request of others by sharing that commitment you have in common and how it will positively impact the greater good of the company or your team.

For example, if you have a complaint about how overtime is starting to burn you out, consider what your commitment is and what your supervisor's goal might be. You are likely to find you both want to complete tasks on time and have quality work product. When you advocate requesting changing the overtime demands, you can say, "I have a goal to have my work done on time and done right. My concern is I am starting to fatigue with the hours and maybe others on my team might feel the same. I worry that the quality and timeliness of the work might start to suffer." Now you and your supervisor can problem-solve based on the commitment (to have quality, on-time work) instead of the complaint (I am working too much and burning out).

To help you find commonalities, here are some commitments that people have for and about their work:

- to have the company be successful
- be successful as an individual
- to have tasks be effective and efficient
- to strive for excellent results and happy clients
- to be recognized for your good work

Take Responsibility for Both What is Working and What Isn't

Responsibility often is considered a negative—in the sense that many people ask who is responsible as a way of finding fault. Consider instead: responsibility is more powerful and positive than that. Responsibility is *the ability to respond*. If your work culture is or isn't working, then everyone in the company has the ability to respond and do something about it. Once you take responsibility and see there is something you can do about the situation, no matter how big or how small, then you can take action to positively impact the environment around you. Without taking action, you will be powerless and a victim of your circumstances.

Take responsibility for fixing the problem with your culture, even if you had nothing to do with causing it. Taking responsibility is not about taking blame. Taking responsibility for your work culture means that you believe you can do something to fix it. By taking responsibility, you declare your commitment to take action and learn from the situation. Only when you take full responsibility and commit to take action can you be empowered as a professional to do your part—to make things work and avoid repeating avoidable issues.

When you have some role in causing the problem, you *do* want to take the blame. It is best if you admit what you did that didn't work, apologize as necessary, and commit both to fixing the situation and learning from it to avoid repeating the problem. This view of challenges and mistakes will give you the confidence to start taking action and seeing how you can move forward.

One Day They'll Carry The Legacy

Jim Collins shared in his book *Good to Great: Why Some Companies Make the Leap . . . And Others Don't* that there are some distinct qualities to the best leaders, the ones who make companies great over time and sustain that greatness.

Collins called these great leaders Level 5 Leaders. A Level 5 Leader:
- Demonstrates humility and a willingness to learn
- Seeks the best for the company even at the sacrifice of his own gain
- Gives others credit for company success and takes full responsibility for failures whether or not he was directly involved
- Works hard and commits to doing what must be done to achieve success

No matter what position you hold in a company, having these qualities will help you and your company succeed. Raise and empower yourself and your employees to become Level 5 Leaders and in time, your culture will be the foundation for the successful company of the future.

Both Jim's book and our book have guidance for company executives. I challenge anyone reading this book to drive all levels of people in the company to learn and exhibit the qualities of a "Level 5 Leader"—and to embrace the task of cultivating the company culture at all points in their career. Be a role model who takes responsibility and advocates for a positive workplace.

You will be a catalyst for work culture greatness.

Everyone can be a part of the solution of a great company culture—or they can be part of the problem.

Which will you choose?

Jen Hamilton

Jen Hamilton is a corporate trainer. For the past five years, she has acted as CEO and principal of her company, Institute for Mastering Success. Companies hire Jen to improve their culture by training staff and management to "play well in the sandbox" and complete their work professionally and punctually.

Jen's work straddles industry and education. She knows what people entering the workforce need to become successful and elevation-ready employees, but she also knows what companies need to foster productivity, professional behavior, and the right attitude. Clients hire Jen to deal with "the jerks at work" and to groom the highest-potential employees.

Jen began her career as a CPA. Her favorite part was not the numbers; it was building great relationships with co-workers, clients, and her bosses. She loves it when her work makes people happy. Atop her CPA work, she volunteered to teach essential professional skills to students and eventually transitioned her career into education. After working with the California Dept. of Education for 7 years, Jen departed to start her own corporate training company. Her background(s) in professional development, volunteer and staff management, and policy and procedure documentation are integral parts of her work in corporate training.

Jen volunteers throughout the community including on two non-profit boards and leading her daughter and niece's Girl Scout troop. She is married to her high school sweetheart and they have two children together. (They're also the humans for two rescue dogs.) Jen enjoys running and the outdoors; given the dry San Diego climate and her tendency to smile throughout her day, she's addicted to Chapstick.

EMAIL jhamilton@InstituteForMasteringSuccess.com
PHONE 858-354-7038
WEBSITE www.InstituteForMasteringSuccess.com
LINKEDIN /in/jenniferdawnhamilton

Michael Harper

Intentionally Cultivating Teams:
Moving Beyond Group Meals and Field Trips

Let me be perfectly clear: I love playing laser tag, driving go-carts at reckless high speeds, and lining up for a huge barbecue buffet with my co-workers. I can also see the value of painting pottery, cooking meals, and going to a ball game together. I am in no way opposed to giving teams a chance to have fun together. Seriously.

BUT—and this is a big but—let's not pretend that these "team-building activities" actually build teams. Building a productive, unified team requires much more than a good meal and a trip to the ballpark.

A Common Misconception

A few years ago, I facilitated a discussion table at a professional conference. The room was filled with Human Resource professionals who, at this particular event, had to quickly decide which topic deserved the next 15 minutes of their lives. They could pick something basic like navigating new insurance laws, or they might branch out a bit and talk about developing their presentation skills. Fortunately, a handful of people felt compelled to join me at my team-building table. My job, then, was to pose the first question, keep the conversation on track, and—of course—keep watch for that one person who always feels the need to dominate the conversation.

Our conversation began with a simple question: What does your company do for team building?

I was surprised at the variety in the group's responses. One by one, the participants proudly listed their company's team-building efforts and how much these efforts are appreciated by their employees. The list included (take a guess):

- A quarterly barbecue lunch with a short motivational speech by the CEO
- A family night at the local minor league ballpark (which also included barbecue)
- An annual trip to play paintball ("the employee team usually beats the manager team!")
- A picnic that includes highly-competitive tournaments with big prizes, such as preferred parking spaces and extra days off from work
- A half-day off for any employee that wants to volunteer at the local non-profit of their choice

My heart sank a bit lower as each person spoke. It sank further still when people started taking notes to remember the "amazing" team building ideas that were being thrown out. Some people even exchanged contact information so they could get outlines and to-do lists from these events.

Here's a question: how does shooting paintballs at your manager build a healthy team? Here's another: how does the reward of a superior parking space and time away from one's co-workers build a team among those co-workers?

And as delicious as it is, what in the world does barbecue have to do with teamwork?

Team Activities vs. Team-Building Experiences

Team activities are fun things that teams do together. Team-building experiences are intentional programs that address your unique team-building goals. Both have value.

Team activities can bond the team by creating shared memories. Used in the right context, these activities can help a team manage stress, celebrate a holiday, or break the monotony of a long workweek. A nicely catered meal can help team members feel valued, which could increase employee engagement. These are smart, mindful activities. But if team activities lack intention, they serve little purpose, and in some cases they can cause unintended damage to the team.

Let's turn some examples around. A catered lunch is a nice gesture, but it doesn't develop teamwork if the employees only sit and eat with the people they already know. Going to a local tourist attraction as a team makes for some great photo opportunities, but does nothing about, for instance, the personality conflicts that are causing the team to miss deadlines. Competitive tournaments may be fun for some, but pitting team members against one another can sometimes bring out the worst in people and easily damage relationships—which will affect the performance of employees much longer than the prizes given out.

Team-building experiences begin with an assessment of the team's specific needs and end with a review of whether the experience will make a long-term difference in the team's ability to hit deadlines, generate revenue, and take care of customers. In the middle, there is an intentional, engaging program that deliberately addresses the issues and behaviors that are preventing the team members from their best performance. These experiences must be results-driven, in a way that justifies the time and money invested to make the program happen.

Calculating Costs
Team-building is much more than connecting employees with those opportunities for personal development. Intentionally building teams increases productivity and revenue; conversely, ignoring interpersonal conflicts and communication problems decreases productivity and revenue. Whether you engage in intentional team-building or a complete lack thereof, it affects the company's bottom line. The question, then, becomes how to engage in team-building experiences that get the best return on your investment.

The word synergy gets tossed around a lot in business circles. It's a word we think we understand and sometimes use to sound knowledgeable. I often hear team leaders and managers say things like:

- I love that my team has synergy. We work together so well!
- Everyone on my team gets along so well. We definitely have synergy.
- We just had a great brainstorming meeting. You can feel the synergy in the room!

The problem with this loaded word is that few people understand what *synergy* actually is. In my seminars, I often ask for someone to define the word. Even when the room is filled with highly-educated people, the definition I usually hear is something like, "Synergy happens when teams work together really well and there's a flow to their work."

Well, sort of.

Synergy is a powerful, transformative word. It's the foundation of teamwork. Synergy exists when two entities work in cooperation with each other to produce a combined effect that is greater than the sum of their parts. In normal math, one plus one is two. In a synergistic relationship, however, one plus one equals much more than two. How much more? It just depends upon exactly how well your team is able to work together.

Understanding the concept of synergy enables us to calculate the value of teamwork—and the money wasted by underperforming teams. When teams lack synergy, they are failing to produce at the level that the company needs them to produce. Failed production leads to lost revenue, right?

Consider these questions when calculating how much money your company is losing to workplace conflict and underperforming teams:

- How often are deadlines missed? How could more aggressive deadlines be met if your team of five people were producing the work of more than five people?
- What is the cost of recruiting and training a new employee? How would creating synergy in your team increase employee engagement and retention?
- What percentage of work is lost due to poor communication and inability to manage workplace conflict?
- How much work are you taking upon yourself because teams are under-performing? How has this affected your work and personal life? How much more productive could your company be if you could focus on business development instead of taking on extra work?

Cultivating a Culture of Team-Building

Once you have a clear picture of how your company's productivity and revenue is affected by teamwork, you can create a plan to cultivate a culture of team-building. Elements of such a plan include:

An Honest Assessment

Determine what your team is currently doing well and where specifically they are struggling. Survey team members to discover their thoughts and feelings about your company's culture in relation to teamwork. Sample survey questions are easily accessible online. In the realm of teamwork, topics such as communication, trust, conflict management, multiple generations in the workplace, time management, personality types, and emotional intelligence often need to be addressed.

A Long-Term, Comprehensive Plan Focused on Results

Teamwork doesn't happen overnight. In fact, we know it takes at least 90 days to change a person's behavior, and much longer than that to change a company's culture. Using the information gathered in the assessment, create a long-term plan broken into realistic steps. Create multiple team-building experiences that address the specific behaviors hindering your team, and make sure that the outcome of each step is clearly articulated.

Company-Wide Buy-In

Shifting a culture requires the entire company to be fully invested, from the C-suite to the interns. Company leadership must send the message, formally and informally, that team-building is vital to the company's success. Employees must understand that developing teamwork skills will positively affect their success in the business world and in their personal lives. Increased teamwork leads to increased revenue, which leads to job security and a positive work environment.

Engaging, Applicable Team-Building Programs

Nothing is worse than being required to attend a team-building day if you feel like your time is being wasted and things will revert to the old ways as soon as the session is over. Team-building programs must be designed to keep participants engaged, and they must be able to show employees how the experience directly connects with their work together. A series of shorter programs scheduled over multiple months works better than a week-long retreat. Convening follow-up sessions within two weeks of a program can help hold team members accountable and help them connect the programs to their day-to-day work together. It is best to bring in an outside facilitator to lead the experiences so that everyone in the company can participate in the experiences together.

Measuring and Adjusting

Be sure the long-term plan for creating a culture of team-building includes regular opportunities for measuring the outcomes of each step and opportunities to adjust the overall plan to meet the company's team-building goals. This includes listening to team members to discover how they responded to the programs; collecting their ideas for improving the team-building experiences; and making sure that the entire company remains focused on the company's team-building goals and how these goals will benefit the company's bottom line.

So What Do You Do for Team Building?

If you ever end up at a professional conference with organized table discussions and you decide to spend a few minutes at the team-building table, be ready to set the record straight. Go-carts and baseball games are fun . . . but cultivating a culture of team building is a much better return on your investment.

Michael Harper

Michael Harper is the owner of Teamworx Talent Development. Michael increases productivity and revenue for companies by decreasing the time wasted by underperforming teams. Michael has more than 20 years' experience developing programs and curricula.

Michael specializes in partnering with professionals to develop their communication skills, self-awareness and team understanding, and work with others. He custom-designs programs that focus on clients' specific team-building needs. It's not about following a curriculum just to follow one; Michael teaches to the company's goal, which often requires original ideas.

All of Michael's programs are interactive—participants are never sitting for long—and focused on active, creative learning. His goal is to have participants transformed by the end of his programs, meaning that they'd consider themselves different people from when they arrived.

Effective teamwork makes a tremendous difference in people's lives. Teamwork strengthens companies; indeed, it's what defines the best companies. Teamwork skills enable each person who has them to find better opportunities in their careers and better relationships in all realms of their lives.

Michael is a native Texan and faithful fan of the Dallas Cowboys. He has been married to his wife Cheri for 20 years and has one daughter. When he's not building teams, you can find Michael riding his bike along the Ohio River, eating Tex-Mex, or sitting around a campfire.

michael@teamworxtd.com
www.teamworxtd.com

Jill Heineck

Beyond the Bottom Line:
How Strong Relocation Strategy Supports a Culture of Innovation and Professional Growth

For many companies, a motivating factor for bolstering internal talent is the competition for top talent. Momentum for talent mobility appears to be growing as companies recognize its mounting relevance in the workplace. So what are the risks if an organization lacks a relocation culture? Its culture must permeate an organization both externally and internally. If you want to be an innovative organization, it stands to reason that your sales process, products, and internal processes must also be innovative. Otherwise, culture will be compromised, half-baked. And culture, like brand, works best when it is consistent.

Ultimately, relocation strategy must be one element that is unified within the cultural values of the organization. It might surprise you to know that many talent mobility teams today are not aligned with the organization's mission, goals, or culture.

To offer employees an authentic and cohesive organizational culture, companies must ensure that their relocation strategies, processes, and technology are aligned with the corporate culture.

To support a culture of innovation, the relocation strategy must offer the latest technologies to employees moving around the world.

To support a culture of flexibility and autonomy, talent mobility must offer programs and processes supporting different employees in a variety of ways.

And finally, to offer a culture of transparency, talent mobility must offer clear messaging throughout the relocation process.

When it comes to relocation (or, as the industry refers to it now, *talent mobility*), eyes roll and expenses quickly add up. Most companies consider relocation a costly but necessary evil to policy and function. However, they fail to see the obvious connection to its talent strategy—which also drives its talent culture. Businesses are so focused on the dollars and cents that they fail to see the investment those dollars and cents could be making. So what happens when the appropriate resources are not allotted to attracting and retaining the best and the brightest? Let's take a look at a company that lost top talent AND an opportunity to build on their culture, all because they could not see the forest for the trees.

A large national food service brand (Company A) was looking to fill a critical role on their leadership team. They found a great candidate and made what they considered a strong offer. But where it excelled as a prosperous career move, it lacked with a measly lump sum for relocation support; it was barely enough to cover the cross-country moving expenses of just the household goods, never mind everything else. Leadership roles imply certain expectations that come with their job offers if relocating is required—whether domestically or internationally. In this case, it appeared to the Candidate that Company A had not done any of its homework about him, his family, his previous relocation requirements, or any of many things that factor into a high-level relocation.

In past leadership roles, the Candidate had been given the proverbial Cadillac of relocation support—and was now instantly repelled by a seemingly insensitive offer. While this was not the Company's intention, it's how it was received. In other words, the first impression to the Candidate was that the Company culture was either non-existent or in disrepair. The first question to cross his mind after their offer was: do they even care about their people? If this is what they do before I even get on the job, what happens 30 or 60 or 90 days in?

The Candidate was also being courted by the Company A's competitor, Company B. While the role was comparable and the comp packages were competitive, the Candidate didn't like Company B's location as well; however, the relocation red carpet had been rolled out for him and his family. Where do you think the Candidate wound up? You guessed it—Company B. Meanwhile, Company A was left reeling: no one in that critical role, a lot of time and resources lost on the process, and for what? To start all over again.

A strong relocation culture lives at the intersection of talent strategy and organizational development—where mobilizing key talent is the key to dynamic business growth. The impact of a strong relocation strategy can result in a shocking amount of return on your cultural investment. Let's face it: your people drive your culture. There are hundreds of stories about companies who lost priceless talent by being cheap and short-sighted; don't become one of them.

A key piece in talent strategy requires having an effective plan to drive organizational culture. If you are building a culture of innovators, then you have to invest in innovators. If you have a culture of data miners, then you have to invest in data miners. Investing in people is how you make this strategy a reality. In today's climate, the need to attract and retain talent is even more important because scouting for outside talent is always more time- and cost-insensitive.

This is where a relocation culture can play another integral role. It can encourage mobility for development and advancement, making it a prime opportunity to build a reputation for clear career paths that include global experience. It's an opportunity for talent leaders to showcase the workplace as an environment built on respect, dignity, and compassion for their workforce. And in turn, the company gains trust of the employees. Over time, the financial returns of companies that experience high trust from their employees consistently outperform their low-trust peers—this is where, in the long run, engagement really is key.

I know, I know, "engagement" is all we hear about these days. But believe some of the hype. Contrary to what some believe, engagement is all your company needs to build the reputation and culture it has always wanted. In simple terms: people just want to feel like they are a part of something. For similar reasons, they want to be informed. The very essence of a reputable company culture lies in its transparency and excellent internal customer service. So what does this look like?

There are three ways talent mobility strategies intersect with organizational culture. First, by having a basic strategy in mind; second, by communicating it; and finally, by being flexible about how it is administered (considering unique needs and adjusting per individual requirements).

Three Ways To Start Somewhere

Let's start with the basics. First, evaluate your talent goals and expectations. Knowing the vision for your talent is necessary before you can set a relocation strategy. Are you lacking in certain areas? What role can relocation play in the company's progress and development?

Next, understand your talent dynamics. Who are the people you will be moving? Are they dual-income families without kids? Domestic partnerships with two dogs? A mom, dad, two kids, and grandma? Two power careers that will require serious convincing and finagling? This information is critical to not only your cost analysis, but also to your approach. Too many times, I have seen companies give employees an ultimatum, essentially, and have it backfire. This kind of thoughtful planning takes time and care up front. Train your team to be more sensitive; really take interest in the human that is considering making a major change in their life to accommodate the company goals. As they say: you catch more flies with honey.

Lastly, benchmark what other companies of your size within your industry are doing (or not doing). What is their average spend for a domestic move for an employee versus a new hire? Homeowner versus renter? How much are they spending on moving the household? How many buy trips do they offer for the family to look for housing? Getting a clear understanding of costs upfront is mandatory to the design of a competitive and cost-effective strategy.

Now Communicate It

Having a succinct communication plan within a relocation strategy may seem like an obvious must, but the lack of a communication plan in some companies is the reason why so many relocations fail, and why so many companies lose millions in the process. The goal is to have humane, informative discussions before a relocation begins. I mentioned "internal customer service" before, and the concept is much the same here as with any good customer service: communicate the message clearly, early, and often.

For your communications, first designate a point person. ONE person. Preferably, that should be a person who likes other people; a person who can empathize with someone uprooting their life and all that goes with it. This may require training in more than one department, not only around what should and should not be discussed, but how that information should be delivered. Sensitivity training might prove beneficial as well. This goes a long way in preserving the integrity of the relocation and protecting the investment.

Next, design an organizational chart for your communication plan: who says what to whom, and when. I promise, this exercise will eliminate so many stressors for your team and relieve anxiety for the employee. Lastly, create a content strategy. Partner with HR or Corporate Communications if you have to, but sit down and collaborate on the messaging you want to deliver before, during, and after a relocation. This is not only to preserve it during the process, but also to create an employee for life. The number one complaint heard from most transferees, and the number one reason relocations fail, is a lack of communication. This is why transparent communication is tanta-mount to the success of any relocation culture. Too often, high-level employees are not informed of their benefits well in advance of transitioning from their old city and role to their new city and role—and they wind up resigning within six months. When that happens, it puts a significant strain on the organization in terms of both time and resources. You have to start over, find a new candidate, spend more company dollars getting them on the job, spend more time ramping them up—it's a mess. And it could all be avoided with a little forethought into how you plan to engage and excite people to work for you.

A C-level executive accepted a key role at a global medical research company. She was super excited and looking forward to her new location, team members, and the work. After just nine months at the company, and more than 150,000 of company cash spent, the executive sadly left her position. Her reasoning? The company failed to communicate with her on multiple levels. The first level was not letting her know who her main point of contact was right away. Seems so simple, right? But too many companies take this for granted and start the employee experience off on the wrong foot.

The second level was not explaining to her the relocation process, her benefits, and how they work. The third breach—and severest of them all—was never answering a call, email or internal IM. She was, essentially, left floundering alone in a new city, new work environment, and new role.

"Setting and managing proper expectations is one of the keys to the employee's success on a new assignment," said Gina Haesloop, former global mobility manager at UPS in Atlanta, GA. "With more than 500 moves per year, UPS is a prime example of how to front-load engagement strategies. A well-designed objective should be known and understood at the beginning of the assignment. That, coupled with periodic feedback, will ensure those identified objectives are in scope," Haesloop adds.

Electrolux is a great example of a masterfully leveraged relocation and communication strategy for retention, engagement, and brand loyalty. When they were making the company move from Augusta, GA to Charlotte, NC, first they sent an invitation to all 400 employees asking them to join the company in Charlotte. Not only was this a brilliant strategic move, it also doubled as an employee engagement opportunity and furthered their employer branding by organically creating brand ambassadors. Employees were flattered to be invited to move with the company and 87% made the move. In addition, every employee had a sufficient time to assess the Charlotte area to be sure it was the right move for them; each had a buy-out (with a cap) as well as flexible benefits based upon their family dynamic. To top it off, employees had a year to utilize a 50% discount on ALL Electrolux appliances to help furnish their new homes.

Do you think they were talking about this grand gesture with their friends, family, and social media circles? Of course! The positive impact on the brand (33% of employees recommend the brand to friends), the continued expansion of the North American head-quarters in Charlotte, and the estimated 810 jobs to be added by 2017 proves that they did. "The program needs to be attractive enough to incent employees to move," said Lee Cibuzar, HR/Benefits Administration Team Leader at Electrolux, "and [it's important] that we look at the employee's move from a holistic perspective."

Be Flexible

Let's face it—we can't be all things to all people. But we sure can do our best to accommodate, right? A huge global hotel company I was working with hired a single homeowner with two pets. The company gave her the same old spiel: "Here is the relocation policy. You fit in Box A, B, or C. Pick one."

She didn't fit in any of them; she was single, with two pets, and going to rent in the new location. She was not going to utilize all the benefits in any box she could pick, so she asked to adjust some of the benefits, but all within the general offer parameters. She was told no. "Do you know how much this policy is worth?" said the Human Resource generalist administering the policy. "It's worth $80,000—so use it or lose it."

There is so much wrong with this. First of all, no HR representative should ever blurt out the cost of the plan to any employee without any kind of framework. Secondly, and yet more importantly, this completely put off the candidate—and as before, immediately gave her a bad omen of things to come working with this company. Needless to say, after six months of company-paid commuting while waiting for her home to sell, she opted to resign, citing "a poor fit" for her.

How hard would it have been to be *just a little bit* flexible with this candidate? $80,000 or not, she was not asking for additional money in this situation. The first way to be flexible is to simply reassign money from one "bucket" or area of the policy to another where it satisfies someone's personal requirements. It would not have cost the company anything but professional courtesy, a bit of time, and perhaps a return on its six-month investment. (For what it's worth: the candidate I mention would have actually *saved* that company about $20,000, or 25% of the cost of the policy, if they'd listened to what she wanted.)

Providing flex services supports individual employees to garner feelings of appreciation, loyalty, and, ultimately, the natural drive to dedicate their best to the company. It's a legitimate part of the workforce strategy.

What are the risks if you don't have a comprehensive engagement strategy that encompasses relocation? According to Nettie Nitzberg, principal at West5 Consulting, "in-boarding" is just as important for an internal employee beginning a new assignment as on-boarding is to a new hire. Nitzberg, who works with global Fortune 500 companies, says that creating an initiative to "on-" or in-board" an employee into the role of their new assignment is a great way to help them acclimate to their new organization or department—creating engagement from the first day and ensuring that the organization realizes a return on their talent investment.

Many times, I am asked how return on investment (ROI) can be measured on relocation programs. To be honest, there is no steadfast way I know to do this. So I asked several companies who are in tune with the relocation process in their companies—almost all said they don't even track it. It might be useful, though, to compare the performance of outsourced labor to performance of in-house labor that is relocated, just as a baseline.

Despite the current state of the economy, global companies still need to lay the groundwork for growth. In doing so, planning for an increase in the mobile workforce is a crucial step toward supporting strategic business objectives. This is where it is critical to connect HR's efforts with talent mobility. After all, without a cohesive, talented team, a company cannot thrive.

Jill Heineck

\

Jill Heineck is arguably one of the most dynamic relocation experts in the industry today. Since graduating Simmons College in Boston, MA with a degree in advertising and PR in 1993, Jill has amassed 20+ years of sales and marketing experience. Prior to real estate, Jill worked in sales and marketing for Fidelity Investments in Boston, in addition to running a successful executive fitness training and wellness practice. With Jill's creative approach, positive personality and marketing background, real estate proved to be the perfect way for her to apply her unique talents and an ideal chance to make a positive difference in the lives of her clients, and of her family and friends. Since joining Keller Williams Southeast as a founding partner in 1999, Jill has experienced great success and grown her business to become widely referred to as the "Relo" expert when it comes to corporate relocation.

In 2002, she earned her Associate Broker designation, and later earned her Senior Certified Relocation Professional (SCRP®) designation. At the 2012 Worldwide ERC National Relocation Conference, she was awarded the prestigious Meritorious Award, as well as Mobility Magazine's Editorial Achievement Award. In 2013, Jill was awarded the Distinguished Service Award, in recognition of her continuous dedicated service and outstanding professional contributions to the global workforce mobility business community.

Aside from her amazing accomplishments in real estate, Jill has become a requested speaker, moderator, and panelist at HR conferences, and industry relocation conferences. Additionally, she has been quoted in the Atlanta Business Chronicle, Atlanta Journal-Constitution, and The Piedmont Review.

A soon-to-be top-selling author, Jill is working on her first book geared to mobile, global organizations.

Relo expert, writer, Realtor®, and cancer survivor, Jill is many things to many people, but above all, she is entertaining, and an inspiration.

Cindy Hines

Working Scared

The atmosphere is different somehow. More doors are closed; shared Outlook calendars now show "private." The senior leadership team seems a little jumpy and short-tempered. Employees are starting to talk about the difference in the air, and without voicing it, they begin to work scared. They go home and tell their spouses or close friends: "I think there is something going on at work. Not sure what it is. But maybe we need to watch our expenses for a while."

Mergers and acquisitions, reorganizations, layoffs, and even shutdowns don't have to be the end of the world. There is life after the company you currently work for. *Right?*

It's hard to stay motivated and productive when you don't have all the information. Without communication, people will make up their own version, and then rumors will fly. It starts innocuously enough, then spreads like wildfire through whispers. *I noticed our industry is declining,* someone thinks. One of the analysts speculates about an M&A; eventually, a key employee leaves for a "better opportunity." *Maybe I should be proactive and start looking for a job,* you think. And before anyone realizes what is happening, there's an entire workforce "working scared" — instead of focusing on running the business.

Fortunately, there are ways to help keep people engaged, and the business running, in the face of ambiguity. Just because life as you know it is about to change drastically does not mean the company culture has to be doom and gloom. Globally, everyone works in a VUCA (Volatile, Uncertain, Complex, and Ambiguous) environment. Organizational change is inevitable, whether via M&As, reorganization, or a declining industry overall.

No matter the reason, communicate the changes as soon as possible, be transparent, help employees stay focused, and treat employees fairly. Some companies wait until the legally-required notice timeframe under the Worker Adjustment and Retraining Notification (WARN) Act to notify the employees who aren't "in the know," or aren't legally required to know. Such organizations seek to protect themselves from a contrived fear of if they know, the world will come to an end. But if employees feel the company and managers don't think they're important enough to know what's going on, they will check themselves out. Conversely, if you show consideration and appreciation toward the employees and explain how their contribution matters, morale will hold steady. People are making life decisions on a daily basis—colleges for children, buying a house, purchasing a car. Providing transparency as early as possible will help employees make informed decisions and be more involved at work, rather than worrying about their future. According to Gallup, 70% of employees are not engaged at work, and it is especially hard on morale when there is a big change initiative.

I've worked for large corporations, and I have personally experienced several reorganizations, three M&As, and two corporate office shutdowns—with few survivors able to move to the new state where the combined US headquarters was located. Before the official notice of one M&A, my husband and I were actively trying to buy a house and had made an offer (which, in a strange twist of luck, was rejected just days before the announcement was made). While we were hopeful that our site would be chosen as the new headquarters, it caused us to hold any thoughts of committing to such a major purchase.

One afternoon, a Human Resource colleague of mine and I were told that a different location was selected as the new US headquarters, and we had to assimilate the information quickly and get through the initial stages of grieving—and rapidly, because the next day was the town hall meeting that would come before the explanation of employees' options. Even though I did not know how this would affect me, personally, at that time I had to be reassuring, supportive, and encouraging. As expected, there were numerous different reactions about continued employment with the company post M&A. Several employees would not consider moving even if given the opportunity; others would consider relocating for the right opportunity; yet others desperately wanted to stay with the organization and were "all in," relocation included.

A few people decided it was in their best interest to go ahead and find a new job rather than wait for the severance package. Which is understandable, but it caused the employees who remained to absorb even more work. One of the ways we helped our employees get through the transition of duties to the new company was to provide internal mentoring and coaching during the wind-down of the old company. While most companies get so wrapped up in the wind-down of the company and put employee development and training on hold, we led an effort to invest in the additional training as support for all employees. We had all of the executive team and some other leaders in the company go through an external workshop to learn how to be better mentors and coaches. We then offered to the headquarters' employees the opportunity to have one-on-one meetings and follow-ups with the trained leaders to support their personal goals. In addition, the coaches and mentors themselves were offered external executive coaching to help them through this trying time. Even the employees who did not choose to participate expressed that it was a good gesture from the company, one they appreciated.

Our Chief Executive Officer was very committed to giving the employees as much information as possible, as soon as possible. We would have frequent town hall meetings where new information was progressively disseminated. Then the Department Heads would have follow-up meetings to answer questions specific to their department. Employees had varying end dates to align with transitioning the business in stages. Because of this open communication, there was a far more trusting environment. We formed an employee group to come up with ideas to keep employees engaged during the lengthy time between the announcement and their scheduled last day. Examples of engagement ideas implemented included onsite yoga and bi-weekly Happy Hour complete with snacks, craft beers, and wine. Casual Friday even turned into casual Monday through Friday (unless you had outside visitors). Instead of cutting back funding on our wellness initiatives, we continued to invest in sponsoring employees in 5K races, incentives for our wellness plan, and a personal trainer for our gym.

It didn't seem respectful to have the usual Christmas party with spouses at a local venue, like we'd had in previous years, so the Wind-Down Committee came up with the brilliant idea to take the Christmas party budget and provide different options to each employee, who could then pick the one that was most appealing to them. Most coordinated the selection with their work friends. Options included NBA tickets, a spa day, deep-sea fishing, a dinner cruise, or tickets to a comedy show. This idea was very well-received as an alternative to the Christmas party.

Each closure in which I was involved was handled differently, and in both instances I felt we treated the employees with respect. We did a lot of good things that I would not change, such as providing a generous severance package (above the national average), a substantial retention bonus, and outplacement support. We had a staged Reduction in Force (RIF), and the substantial retention bonus was offered in addition to the severance if the employees stayed until the designated date. Only a few employees tested their luck to see if they could "quit and stay" by doing the minimum to get by. This was followed with a conversation where we explained we still had a business to run and if they wanted to receive their retention bonus and severance that they should continue to devote their best efforts. Fortunately, we never had major issues with that. The outplacement support we provided was through an outside Human Resources firm that specializes in career transitions. In total, this was above and beyond the services to which employees are entitled when companies close under WARN.

We did a lot of things right, but there were a few things that could have been better—such as actively combining the cultures, which proved successful in a previous M&A. Another time, the decision was made to have the transferred people adapt to the existing culture, rather than start a new combined culture, because why should anything change? We have been successful thus far. But often, that mentality causes the newly-relocated employees to feel like outsiders, which adds difficulty adapting. Many already feel a little survivor's guilt because so many of their former colleagues did not stay with the company. To ease the transition, we learned along the way to align benefits and compensation as soon as possible, so you don't have people working side by side who receive drastically different benefits and compensation.

Another great practice is to have at least one person on the HR team who is a part of the work stream coordinating the employees who are transferring, and another person on the HR team focused on those leaving. This proved to be a very smart idea, as the person responsible for "leavers" was also exiting and was able to empathize with their situation, just as the HR team member in charge of transfers was transferring and able to fully focus on their successful transfer to the new company.

There was another time in my career that we had two weeks to notify and lay off approximately 200 employees who did not fall under WARN. We had all hands on deck, with phone trees and talking points prepared. We were able to take care of everyone, without any legal entanglements, and our HR team received global recognition with an organizational effectiveness award. Yet this award, while complimentary to our team, did not compensate for the heartache we felt when we had to tell our co-workers goodbye.

I know what it is like to work scared when you don't know what the future will bring. After all, I was one of the 300+ employees who was laid off. But I found that, with a generous severance package, frequent open communication, some low-cost fun activities, and genuine care and compassion for those being laid off, it can actually become a positive transition in life.

I found that, in most cases, employees were able to find equal or better jobs, with the same or better salaries. They were able to spend more time with loved ones; some were able to reinvent themselves by pursuing an entirely new passion. For example, an outside salesperson who had left employment a couple of months before beamed at me and said, "It has been a blessing to have been given this paid time off to figure out the next phase of my life. I am teaching part-time at the local college, taking an art class, volunteering at my children's school, and my wife and I are able to spend more time together."

Seeing him happy, I began to realize that working scared can be transformed into a transaction of gratitude—with the right planning and support, and with fairness from the company and its leaders.

In closing, please be reminded of your responsibility. You may not have the budget, or even the support of management, but it is an ethical imperative for you to do everything you can to lessen what hurts in this time. Be there for the employee; coach, counsel, offer assistance, meet with families, and use your network to help place people. Remember to pay it forward!

ABOUT THE AUTHOR

Cindy Hines

MBA, SPHR, SHRM-SCP

Cindy Hines is a Strategic Human Resource Advisor for HRD Strategies, Inc. She began this position this year, in 2016, after an M&A.

Cindy brings experience from the fast-moving consumer-goods industry, healthcare, and banking, plus domestic, multi-state, and international experience—all focused on shaping the HR agenda to support key organizational goals.

Cindy has been involved in several organizational restructurings and M&As (mergers and acquisitions). She focuses on change management within her work. She will be teaching management and human resources part-time at Western Kentucky University beginning in the Spring of 2017.

This is Cindy's second professional anthology—to read her previous work, check out *What's Next in Human Resources* from Greyden Press.

In her free time, Cindy enjoys time spent on the water kayaking and boating. She has been married to her husband John for 31 years, and together they have two daughters and two canine kids.

EMAIL cynthiavhines@gmail.com
WEBSITE www.hrdstrategies.com
LINKEDIN /in/cindyhines

Mark Leonardi

Beat to a Different Drum

Big or small, all companies have a culture—and culture is the driving force that separates high-performing companies from mediocre ones.

Culture can be a competitive advantage—or it can be abused and neglected by leaders. Your working culture is defined by thousands of interactions that happen every day among employees. A recent survey by Glassdoor found that 90 percent of employees surveyed would consider leaving their current jobs if offered another role at a company with a more positive reputation. **It's culture that attracts and retains talent.** It is a form of energy in constant motion that cannot be stored, but can be used where it exists to lift an organization up—or in the wrong hands, a culture can inhibit an organization's growth, or simply remain untapped.

Over the past decade, many companies have turned to employee recognition to engage their workforces and adapt themselves to a changing economy. With pay raises being fewer and employee workloads often increasing, recognition can enhance employee engagement and strengthen an employee's emotional connection to an organization. Many studies point to the benefits of recognition on employee retention and, even better, creating a sense of belonging. People are less likely to leave a company, by over two times, when they receive recognition, compared to people in similar positions who do not receive recognition.

Recognition is an excellent communication tool, and it supports performance management. Showing people you care about them and that you are active in their success will lead to higher performance from them. Positive energy from recognition creates a culture of appreciation—and people want to be part of this kind of emotional connection.

Consider the large (and growing) Millennial workforce and their typical need for ongoing feedback and development. Recognition provides them with the catalyst to provide this feedback to you. The ability to attract, retain, and grow this younger talent as the workforce faces many retiring Baby Boomers means that recognition has become an essential tool for leaders to energize an organization.

How can recognition make a difference in your organization? At a large global restaurant company I know, it was recognition efforts in particular that ignited a team across many business units and geographies. This company was seeking to define its identity more clearly, having followed a spin-off and become a publicly traded company. The leadership team wanted to create a culture where all people mattered. Celebrating the achievement of others is still their formula today, and it has ignited passion to accomplish real and tremendous results. Leaders there demonstrated, in a personal way, that recognition can make a difference in people's lives each day. As the positive energy of the organization came alive, a passion to make a difference became evident in the employees and in the great customer experiences they were able to provide. The power to put a smile on a customer's face can only come alive if employees feel engaged and empowered to make that difference for someone else.

My personal journey with recognition at the restaurant company began with the beat of a drum: a personal passion to lift the spirits of my fellow employees. Our leaders were gracefully exemplifying a culture of recognition. The message in every meeting and workshop was the power of teamwork. We consistently recognized the achievements of others. Whether it was a small win along the way or the support you may have received from another employee, you quickly became aware of your ability to show appreciation; that became the mindset.

Spontaneous recognition would occur regularly in the office or within one of our own restaurants. Our CEO would lead the way and he even created his own recognition award: instead of the usual plaque, he gave out a rubber chicken with a handwritten note on it and made it fun, complete with a photo with the employee. He proudly lined the walls of his office with photos of every person he'd recognized. Soon enough, the walls were filled—so he put more framed photos on the ceiling! Needless to say, when you went to his office, you felt the power of recognition and the genuine appreciation for people across the company. The halls of the building followed suit with pictures lining the halls of people who were recognized. You could not help but feel emotionally connected and even inspired just as you walked around the building.

I personally felt compelled to take recognition to the next level and the crazy idea to form a recognition band came to life. With no musical ability to speak of, a few employees and

I formed the Random Acts of Recognition Band. I rented a big bass drum, and along with fellow employees who knew how to play a saxophone and guitar, the band was formed. We would accompany leaders marching the halls of our office, or bust into a meeting to recognize an employee. We would gather other employees as we marched through the building on our way to someone's office to surprise them. Imagine the beat of a drum in the hallway as you are working in your office. There was magic in the fact that people would hear the Random Acts of Recognition Band coming, and they would come out of their offices to join the march to see who was being recognized. People would clap to the music and our recognition song would always end with *we are here to recognize YOU!* as we arrived to the surprise of the employee being recognized. The employee would be greeted with smiles, laughter, and a whole-hearted sense of "thanks."

As they were told why they were being recognized, people would cheer and the employee would receive a personal recognition award from the person who had submitted the recognition. The challenge that every employee should have their own personal recognition award came from the CEO—and employees enjoyed being creative with their award and sharing their gratitude toward others.

Recognition can have a profound effect on the culture and overall engagement level of an organization. The ability to lift people up, in both business and in life, is sorely needed in today's businesses and society. With the overwhelming positive effect of recognition, today's leaders are not beating the drum—and in some cases, they are simply beating people down. Recognition has been shown to improve employee engagement and lower employee turnover by over 30%. According to the US Department of Labor, 64 percent of working Americans leave their jobs because they do not feel appreciated.

Celebrating the accomplishments of others is a leader's responsibility if they want to inspire their people and create a positive culture. Appreciating and recognizing successfully can be accomplished with the following thoughts in mind:

- **Be authentic and show you care.** Saying "great job, but" negates any positive behavior you were trying to reinforce. Know how each person on your team likes to be recognized, whether publicly or more privately. Know what their favorite candy bar or restaurant is. Make recognition personal!
- **Be specific.** Describe the "what" and "why" behind the recognition. It should be clear what was accomplished and how it made a difference to someone. As an example: saying "Sally led the way to reduce turnover in the division" does not

provide enough context. But it's great to hear about Sally's ability to revamp the onboarding experience, how her work conducting stay interviews and manager training reduced turnover by 20 percent. It sounds more like an accomplishment when you're specific about the efforts and rewards.

- **Be spontaneous.** Recognize when you see the right thing happening. Do not wait until the next quarterly meeting to recognize that action. Leverage different communications to make the recognition come to life in a timely way. On the other hand, just be careful; if recognition is a bullet point on every meeting's agenda, it may come across as a "check the box" item that doesn't get full dignity or attention.
- **Encourage recognition up, down, and across.** Model recognition as the leader while supporting appreciation to and from all levels of the organization. I can personally speak to the power of recognition to senior leadership when I recognized the CEO on behalf of the organization with his very own rubber chicken award.

There is no substitute for a CEO who can lead the way in driving a recognition culture. If your CEO is considering hiring a "Chief Engagement Officer," then the CEO is likely not invested to personally make a difference. The success of a recognition program must be led by example from the CEO and leadership team—not a newly invented position. When setting the strategy, recognizing and motivating employees is often an overlooked element of the strategy. Many leaders point to incentive plans to say how they are motivating their people—but incentives are different from recognition. In short, recognition focuses on the how and incentives focus on the what. Metrics and quantifiable goals are essential to an organization, of course, but by focusing on behaviors, an organization can move forward more quickly. It's a healthy balance of incentives and recognition that seems to provide an employee the best rewards for their positive results.

When designing a recognition program, you should consider the following:

- Is there senior leadership support? If so, how do we know? If not, what steps are necessary to engage leadership?
- What values in your organization "speak to" rewarding and recognizing people consistently?
- What resources, budget, and training may be necessary to get a recognition program started?

- How will the success of that recognition program be measured? Is there a balance between incentives and recognition programs?
- What is the communications plan, and how will periodic feedback be gathered from employees? How are you getting input?

According to Gallup, 69 percent of employees prefer appreciation and recognition to financial rewards, and 82 percent say that recognition inspires them to improve their performance. This data suggests that organizations should consider a harder look at recognition and the way they tend to incent their employees. On the flip side, research suggests that some financial incentive programs discourage teamwork, creativity, and the delivery of the best solution to the customer.

Are we paying attention to what actually motivates and connects emotionally with the employees in today's workforce? Doing what has been done in the past isn't a strategy for future success. The courage to ask employees and listen to their feedback is one of the first things you need in building a recognition culture. Listening is recognition. You are acknowledging their abilities and talents; they appreciate the fact that you asked for their input, that part of your job is to act on their feedback. When culture is emotionally connecting to your team, employees respond by knowing the what and how for getting things done. Teams work across functions and challenge one another to challenge the status quo. Energy is not wasted on the what's in it for me mentality; instead, positive energy stays in the organization, and as it spreads, everyone pulls for everyone else to succeed.

I am always amazed by the power of the human spirit and how simple acts of kindness and positivity can impact our life. I recall a friend, Steve, who was told by his doctor that he only had a few days to live after battling cancer for over a year. With the help of a family friend, Steve received a surprise visit from a pro football player he idolized—and his enthusiasm for life was re-energized. The athlete was also inspired by Steve's passion for life and continued to visit him weekly. They shared their past and formed a lasting connection. Sadly, Steve passed away six months later. Still, the doctors were astonished and attributed his longevity to the compassion and caring he received, not only from his family and friends but also from his idol. Steve always looked forward to those weekly visits and to seeing his idol and friend again. Steve's experience provided me an insight to the positive effect we have on one other. Or, how we can minimize one other with our careless words or actions?

In the April 2016 Harvard Business Review article "Culture is Not the Culprit," the authors suggest culture is not something you "fix." Rather, they explain, cultural change is "what you get when you put new processes or structures in place to tackle tough business challenges." A recognition strategy is a tool that leaders are leaving in the shed and not leveraging to build collaboration, trust, and innovation. Leaders need to demonstrate passion—and they need to use two simple, powerful words: **thank you.**

What are you doing to beat the drum in your organization?

ABOUT THE AUTHOR
Mark Leonardi
MS

Mark Leonardi is Director, Associate Services for ORR Corporation in Louisville, KY. He is a collaborative leader who seeks to bring out the best in teams. He leads by communicating a clear HR vision to instill a culture of effectiveness and engagement.

Mark is passionate about coaching senior leaders to deliver an engaging, inclusive culture where associates feel valued to drive innovation and high performance. By listening to associates' voices, Mark instills trust and respect for others to deliver positive business results with an outstanding customer experience within the organization.

Mark's experience began at PepsiCo and then moved to Yum! Brands and Fifth Third Bank. He is currently leading human resources at ORR Corporation, a growing safety and fire suppression organization. His areas of expertise include employee engagement, emotional intelligence, leadership and organizational development and talent management.

Mark is a "wellness activator" and has been a lifelong supporter of wellness initiatives and programs. He has received extensive training in Emotional Intelligence and Coaching for Intentional Development through Case Western Reserve University.

EMAIL markleonardi518@gmail.com
LINKEDIN /in/markleonardi

Nicole Price

Culture Room by Room:
The 3 Ps of Placing Leaders Well

"Everyone is a genius. But if you judge a fish by its ability to climb a tree, it will spend its entire life thinking it's stupid."
— **ALBERT EINSTEIN** —

I believe that all leaders can be great—not some, but all. There is a common belief that leaders are born; we say that leaders can be made, but we don't act like we believe it. If we truly believed leaders could be made, why did we allow leadership to be one of the few positions a person is allowed to hold without any training? A person isn't permitted to drive a city bus without training, but people are placed in management roles every day who have not been given any true knowledge of what their role entails.

Why does this matter in a book about cultivating culture? Because culture is broad, and because trying to change culture is often like standing inside a house but complaining about the weather outside. The key to success, at that level where most of us work, is to focus on the thermostat in the room—the leader. Leaders control the "temperature" of the microclimates in our organizations. They hold the key to the thermostat. If you've ever worked for a less-than-stellar company but had an excellent leader, you know what I mean; you likely enjoyed your daily work and looked past the faults of the company because your leader was the person who had a direct impact on what your work climate was like each day. Conversely, if you've ever worked inside an amazing company but had a horrible leader, you know exactly what I mean here, too. Individual leaders determine the culture for the vast majority of an organization's employees.

I was one of those leaders who (unknowingly) created a microclimate that wasn't great for my direct reports. At the time that I transitioned into leadership, I was in a manufacturing role. Unlike some people in my field, I did receive some foundational supervisory courses like FMLA, HIPPA, Union Relationships, and so forth. But I did not receive any true leadership training until almost a year into the assignment, and the people following me suffered. The lack of training wasn't the only reason for the breakdown . . . as it turned out, my personality was another!

The explanation has its beginnings early in my life. As a young person, I was naturally gifted in science and in mathematics, so I was encouraged to be an engineer. While working as an engineer and leading a team of technical professionals, I received an offer from the Human Resources (HR) department to conduct what they called a "high performance workshop"—their euphemism for "your team is dysfunctional and we are here to help sort it out." This workshop would use an assessment tool to help me, as a leader, learn to work better with my direct reports. The workshop would also help build trust on my team. One thing was for sure: I didn't trust several of my team members. So I willfully agreed to the help.

At the high performance workshop, HR facilitated several exercises with my team using the Myers-Briggs personality instrument. They had several fun activities that helped us see how we each approached issues like change management, communication, decision-making, and conflict. The interesting thing was that, for each one of the topic areas except for decision-making, my team was in lockstep and I was the odd person out. For the first time in my life, I had a major work-interest epiphany: it really wasn't them, *it was me!*

Looking back on my life in engineering school, I should have seen it. When I look back at pictures, it was visible even in the way I dressed. Although I loved engineering work, my personality completely disagreed with it. HR was swift to assign me an executive coach so that I could adjust my style and improve the work climate around me.

While I was able to make the adjustments, it was hard for me to lead in that environment. It was like brushing my teeth with the opposite hand. It was inauthentic, awkward, forced. What do you think that did to my own personal microclimate? My personal engagement was low, so how could I effectively inspire others?

That experience has certainly shaped my leadership philosophy. After my first coaching experience, I've thought about leadership style a lot. It was that experience that created my desire to help the world understand something: just how important it is to fit the leader to the role that's appropriate for them. When leaders set out to inspire and engage others, it isn't just business. It is personal.

Leaders rely on their personal methods for:
- Setting direction,
- Inspiring others to follow, and
- Driving for positive outcomes.

These same leaders depend on a wide range of abilities, such as dealing with ambiguities, communicating vision and purpose, leveraging strengths, capitalizing on change, and maintaining effective working relationships (which includes conflict management). The way each individual approaches these topics is largely based on personality style. I have conducted my share of 360-degree reviews of leaders, and many times I can decipher a leader's personality type based simply upon the competencies in which he or she rates highest and lowest. This is because, even if you stretch yourself to learn new behaviors, your greatest assets will remain your greatest assets and your weaknesses will rarely become strengths.

Marcus Buckingham has been telling us this for years, but it was never more real for me than the time I found my old workbook from when I'd attended a Stephen Covey workshop in 1994. Decades later, I was still great at the same things and still working on the same weaknesses. Even as a self-proclaimed exemplar of self-improvement, I am not different in this way.

What does this mean for culture? It means we need to assess the leadership style of our people when we place them in leadership assignments. A person who is a great plant manager might not have the temperament to lead the company's foundation; in general, the ideal personalities are different for each of those roles. Let's be clear: I am not suggesting that personality should be used as a screening tool, as a primary criterion for job placement. But I am saying that, in addition to offering foundational leadership training, knowing a person's leadership style could mean the difference between a leadership role which is a good fit for the leader and an asset to the business—or a long spell of struggle and misunderstanding.

People are more than names in the proverbial 9-box that we move around like chess pieces. We have the ability to ask them about their personal interests (among many other things). If leadership is anything at all, it is personal. So what can we do to make use of that?

The Three P's – Purpose, Passion, Prowess

Purpose

Ask leaders to reflect on what they love to do, where they like to do it, and with whom they like to do it. Sometimes people land in leadership roles because they were talented doers. That doesn't mean that they can't be exceptional leaders, but sometimes they should be asked whether or not they want to leaders, truly. Leadership is hard work; it is not for the faint of heart. One must be willing and able—but to do that work in particular. The same person who leads well in a correctional facility may not be the same person to lead in a private school. In similar ways, leading a startup is not the same as leading an established Fortune 500 organization. Again, the key is to align individual leadership purpose with the right working culture.

For many leaders, purpose is hard to identify at times because, when a person is aligned to their "purpose work," the work seems to be done effortlessly. Encourage leaders at all levels to consider what people always lean on them for, to identify what they make time for even when they're super-busy. They may not have considered that that's what they could be doing with their whole life.

You will find that some leaders decide that leadership in your organization is not for them. That is perfect when it happens. When considering culture, the first requirement is commitment; a natural filter for that culture, therefore, is to willfully allow the uncommitted to find something else to which they can commit.

Passion

Engagement is inevitable when passion is part of the work. Do you want an engaged culture? Align leadership passion to the work. Ask your leaders: "What's the work you'd do for free?" When Gallup defines engagement, one of the critical components is discretionary effort—how much effort do people give of their own volition?

Passion fuels the effort engine. Passion is what keeps you going when others would get tired and quit. Leaders have a unique challenge; they have to worry specifically about engagement, not only engagement from others but engagement from themselves. Passion provides leaders with the sincerity to show up every day with the energy they need for their own work and have enough left over to lead their team.

I have asked thousands of leaders what gets in the way of their effectiveness as leaders. One answer that always makes the list is "lack of time." When you are leading others, the meetings and decisions and performance reviews (and everything else) chip away at the clock. If they fall into this endless routine, where their passion diminishes, leaders grow tired. Weariness and fatigue can be combated by making sure people are working in areas where they have passion, where they continue to find energy.

Prowess

What do a day laborer and a new leader have in common? In either case, people assume that you don't need more than a day's worth of knowledge to get the job done. While that might work among unskilled workers, it is not a great strategy for appointing leaders. After all, they hold the key to the thermostat for everyone.

Leadership skill is imperative. It's not always enough to know a leader's purpose and passion. If purpose and passion do not overlap with your skill, there will still be failures. When discussing culture change, teaching leaders to effectively coach is a good part of the discussion for mitigating the risk of failure. However, I've noticed that we're unclear about what coaching is and what it isn't. I have participated in hour-long coaching conversations with my leader . . . about her dog.

And, sadly, my experience is not that uncommon.

Alan Fine at InsideOut Development has created one of the most comprehensive coaching approaches I've used. He breaks down which coaching conversations to have and when. However, Fine does something else that is critical. He delineates when coaching is necessary and when advice-giving is necessary instead. Sometimes there are knowledge gaps. This is especially true in . . .

- new leadership situations,
- transitions from being a technical professional to being a leader,
- people working in a new leadership environment, and
- people new to middle or senior leadership.

It is not always a knowledge issue, but sometimes it is. What does this mean for you if you are trying to cultivate culture? Acknowledge that there is a leadership learning curve that needs to be addressed in each of the transitions. It is estimated that the average person needs to put in 10,000 hours of practice to develop mastery of something. Why would leadership be different? We have to give leaders on-the-job training opportunities and close their skill gaps at every level of leadership. This is an essential step for building solid leadership within any company.

Let's say you have the three Ps covered—purpose, passion, and prowess—and there is still a leadership issue. What then? The culprit is likely accountability.

Accountability

You can't have a culture discussion without the word "accountability" entering the conversation. So here's my twist: at the turn of the 20th century, C.H. Turner conducted an experiment with fleas that now helps me to explain accountability.

If you put fleas in a glass, they jump out. But if you put fleas in a glass and put a lid over that glass, the fleas will jump and hit their bodies against the lid until they realize it hurts. At that point they will start to jump just below the lid. Once all the fleas are jumping just below the lid, the lid can be removed and the fleas will never jump out of the glass.

Why not? Because they have learned to be helpless. They tried really hard in the past and experienced painful failure, so much failure that now they imagine obstacles that don't actually exist and lack the self-assuredness to live fully as they were designed—as incredible jumpers (who'd always been capable of jumping out of the glass).

This phenomenon is the opposite of accountability, and it is called learned helplessness. Leaders experience learned helplessness, too. Over my experiences, I have learned four distinct principles to help leaders overcome learned helplessness and step into the power they (already) have to lead their whole lives well.

The Four Principles Against Learned Helplessness in Leadership

1. All leaders can be great leaders within their unique leadership purpose. (All fleas can jump out of the glass naturally.)

Sometimes our leadership challenges are not skill issues. Our leaders have the prowess or skill. Do we believe they have the skill? We have to buy in to the belief that 100% of leaders can be great at leadership under the right circumstances. We first have to believe in our own innate ability to make a personal difference in the world with something unique; sometimes we find that something and other times it finds us. Regardless, I believe that every person has a unique gift or calling.

2. Sometimes, a person or system will place a "lid" or obstacle in our way. Leaders need to have a mindset shift in these situations. We don't have perfect leadership environments; no one operates in a vacuum. If you can only lead well when you are perfectly aligned to your purpose, when you have all the skills for the job—or only when you are incredibly passionate about the work—that is not helpful. If this were the case, my belief that 100% of leaders could be great wouldn't be tested every day, like it is (I said I believed it, but I never said it was watertight). Leaders have to have the resolve to be great even in less-than-ideal circumstances.

3. Those of us with power, privilege, and influence have a responsibility to help remove lids for others. What are our the "lids" we place on leaders that prevent them from stepping fully into their roles? What are the ways that we can break down those barriers to create space and freedom for people to be able to lead in different ways, ways that better meet the needs of their specific work group or area? We have a responsibility to remove obstacles when we see them. This is especially important when we're in positions of power. It is easy to tout accountability when you are outside of the glass—but what are you doing to help those who are inside the glass?

If we are going to do anything to impact the persistent leadership challenges that plague our organizations and hinder our culture efforts, we have to include in the conversation our proverbial Lid Removal Plan.

4. Open your mind to the possibility that old obstacles are not challenges today. Sometimes there is no lid and we're simply imagining one. What are your leaders doing incredibly well? What are the ways you can build on those strengths? Imaginary lids are sometimes the hardest to break through, and that's because they work in our minds, where we generate our efforts and motivations. We are hardly a match for the power of our own minds. Just for today, imagine that none of your leaders have skill problems. What if their issue is simply a lack of self-assuredness? If that's the case, what can we do to build the confidence of our leaders?

Now What?

"Start where you are. Use what you have. Do what you can."
— ARTHUR ASHE —

Are you behind the eight-ball with your leadership training—or, worse, are you investing tons of money in leadership development training and seeing no results? Remember to be kind to yourself. Remember, too, that while you're trying to create a longer-term strategy, you'll still need somewhere to start.

One good starting point is lunch-and-learn sessions (in-person or virtual). At one such session, you could take one of numerous useful personality assessments (Colors, Tilt, MBTI, DISC, and so on) that can be used to assess leadership styles within the group. Bring your leaders together after completing an assessment; then, within their "style groups," have them say aloud what they intend to give people with other styles and what they might need from others. Given the professional-but-informal tone at many lunch-and-learns, it's a good idea to use them to share information about compassionate leadership, conflict management, change, decision-making, and any other leadership training that might move your culture in the right direction. This simple approach will help to build trust within your culture.

Remember that I am here to help, too! Please feel free to contact me using the information on the next page if you'd like to brainstorm options and solutions for your own organization.

Nicole Price

Nicole Price gets it.

She understands that if leadership is anything, it is personal, and that everyone can be a great leader — everyone can lead his or her own, whole life. So she gets personal. Nicole's transparency allows others to learn from her mistakes and helps them avoid the same pitfalls. She gets real. She will tell you, yes, having differences within a team can be harder, but that hard work can really pay off — both professionally and personally. And she gets wise. She'll tell you, in a heartbeat, how she's gotten a few things wrong over the years, but a little grace and some solid coaching saved her.

Can you make mistakes and still be an awesome leader? Is it possible to lead effectively with so many personalities on one team? Can you genuinely lead people and still have a decent life and energy left to live it? If you ask Nicole, the answer is absolutely yes.

Through leadership development, coaching, consulting, keynotes, and other resources, Nicole encourages and enables others to live their lives in excellence. Her energetic and engaging sessions leave participants with strategies and specific tools that they can apply right away. Her lively presentation style garners rave reviews and, very often, an invitation to return.

Nicole received her B.S. in chemical engineering from North Carolina A&T University and her master's degree in adult education from Park University. For more information about Nicole and Lively Paradox programs, please visit www.livelyparadox.net.

Cheryl Schofield

Toward a Culture of Positivity

There are many benefits to cultivating a culture of positivity, and they're worth considering. After all: who among us prefers to work in the *opposite* kind of culture?

Recall a time when you were perhaps tethered, however temporarily, to a toxic place. The resulting stress, dissatisfaction, and negative emotions can seriously impact one's health and well-being. Not to mention that, in turn, this affects organization performance and productivity.

While facilitating an off-site business meeting for a consulting project, I had an unexpected—and unpleasant—encounter with a stranger in attendance. There was a misunderstanding, she quickly passed judgment on me, and she made a serious allegation against me. Confident in my innocence, I calmly stated such and elected not to give the issue any attention, to remain focused instead on what I knew were the positive aspects of my work. The following day, the situation was cleared up and my innocence was confirmed. Although this person had publicized my alleged guilt, and not offered an apology, she later wanted to befriend me. Practicing positivity and mindfulness, I chose to focus on what went right and to be receptive to my accuser's newfound interest in connecting with me. All ended well when it might not have.

In my coaching and consulting practice, a number of clients are seeking to make career moves. Often, the person describes their desire to escape an unfavorable situation with their manager, their department, or their perceived culture. One young woman was so desperate to flee her department (bad boss, high turnover, and overwork) that she was prepared to leave *before* securing another position—risking a loss of income and benefits.

So, what constitutes a culture of positivity? The relatively new realm of positive psychology offers a good deal of research.

Psychologist Barbara Frederickson has extensively examined *positivity*, or the study of positive emotions. Her research shows that people who experience positivity have increased creativity, flexibility, resilience, and a bigger-picture perspective. They tend to become better versions of themselves. Although there are many, Frederickson focuses on ten positive emotions that include joy, hope, inspiration, and gratitude. Positive emotions broaden one's thinking and build psychological resources. Engaging in practices that produce employees' positive emotions helps shape a culture of positivity. There is a ripple effect; people's emotions are contagious, and this is especially true of leaders' emotions.

I have a memorable experience that might provide an example. I was consulting for a company that was having a large gathering of about 800 employees at a hotel for a national meeting. (So you can picture it: the gender composition of this group was about 90% male, given the industry.) Tragically, one of the employees in attendance suffered a massive heart attack one night in his room and died. Naturally this was a very serious event, handled with due diligence and respect by the HR staff and company executives.

The following morning, in the large ballroom where the meeting was held, one leader to whom the deceased man's team reported talked briefly about the man's passing, offering an emotionally-charged impromptu speech in his honor and then observing a period of silence in memoriam. Company representatives quickly assembled a small memorial on site at the hotel and ensured there was grief counseling available for anyone interested. In numbers I'd never seen before, I observed grown men reach out to each other in tears, embracing in hugs of comfort. As part of the memorial with the employee's picture and an arrangement of flowers, there was a journal for people to offer their thoughts. Numerous men wrote in the journal.

The actions of the primary leader, who had initiated a dedication to the deceased employee, opened the door for others to allow themselves to be vulnerable and express their grief. This leader modeled sincere feelings of connection to this valued employee, permitting others to do the same. Although I did not personally know the man, I was moved by the whole experience, realizing once again the value of positive emotions like hope and inspiration, and appreciating the value of connections and relationships. The experience was powerful and empowering at the same time that it was sad. Part of the value of positivity is that other people seem to follow suit when one person opens up and shares. It was heartening and made a positive impression on many.

Not all examples in the workplace environment are positive, of course. I am reminded of an experience when working in a large corporation, where the employees around me were impacted on a regular basis by deadlines, lack of role clarity, and disparity in the workload distribution. As a Human Resources leader, I interfaced not only with members of my own team, but also with managers and other leaders in the organization. Often they lamented having to do someone else's work, about their dilemma: how, if they waited on the person responsible, their own work and deliverables would be negatively impacted, but they didn't feel it was right to have to do the other person's work, essentially "letting them slide."

Although I empathized, generally my response was, "Do you want to be right, or do you want to be effective?" After all, they were right. But if they really wanted to do their own work effectively, perhaps they were going to have to do "more than their share."

Indeed, I experienced some of the same things myself; usually I urged laggards to do their work and carry their share, but in the end I wanted to get the job done well. So I chose to do more than what was expected. In order to do this without the frustration or bitterness one might expect of the situation, I found the general tenets of positivity useful. Positivity opens us up. Positive emotions expand our peripheral vision, helping us to see the big picture and the interconnectedness of systems. People are more likely to be resilient, more trusting, and to look past differences to oneness.

Let me be clear: I'm not advocating that we should simply let others at work "get away with" doing less on a regular basis. Rather, the point is to teach and use positivity as a tool. The plain reality is that people do contribute to different degrees at different times. Some people give 85% and others seem to give 120%, and it might change day by day (or it might not). When we want to take control of maintaining our own effectiveness, and that happens to require we do more than our share, employing the practice of positivity can be helpful.

Challenges like these might sometimes seem relentless and eventually leave us feeling helpless. But in every challenge there's an opportunity—if we choose to remember it and think of it that way. Reframing can make all the difference in turning something negative to positive. Jim Loehr and Tony Schwartz, in their book *The Power of Full Engagement*, call this recasting. Reframing and recasting simply create a different perspective designed to better serve us. These authors also discuss the importance of managing energy, with an emphasis on a balance between expenditure and renewal. Restoration is another idea in the toolkit for improving employees' positivity.

University of Michigan business school professor Kim Cameron studies positive leadership and organization virtuousness. His research shows that a leader's positive energy significantly increases employee job satisfaction, well-being, performance, and engagement—all reasons to teach and encourage business leaders to practice positivity. Positive leaders are genuine, trustworthy, and dependable, and they energize others. A leader's positive energy is four times more powerful than typical characteristics of leadership influence. One person makes a difference that affects many.

Meaning and purpose is a cornerstone for positivity. People seek meaningful connections, which lead to positive emotions. Helping employees understand and connect to the greater vision and mission of an organization can assist them to begin thinking of obstacles as prospects, with hope for achieving the vision shared by other members of the group. Having that unified, clear vision and helping people see the linkage of their own roles to that vision offers a sense of meaning and purpose to their work, whatever it might be. A lack of clarity about the vision—about the reason for being there—often creates a consistent negative impact, while a shared vision generates more positive emotions.

Helping others stimulates positivity. Research by psychologist Jonathan Haidt shows that givers and receivers of help tend to experience positive emotion as a result of the interchange—and remarkably, people who merely hear about the helping event also feel positive emotions, even though they were not involved. This is called *elevation*.

It brings to mind recent discoveries about the effect of brain cells called *mirror neurons*, whereby we immediately and instinctively understand and empathize with the thoughts, feelings, and intentions of others simply by witnessing an event or incident, although we are not directly involved. Surely there is potential for the application of elevation in organizations. The power of story-telling, eliciting some kind of feelings from the audience, could facilitate the effects of elevation.

So, what can organizations do to cultivate a culture of positivity?

As I mentioned, leaders can model inspiration, instill hope, and behave in ways that demonstrate and stimulate positive emotions. **In short: be authentic.** Communicate the vision honestly so that employees understand how their work contributes to it in a meaningful way.

Practice compassion—a quality that certainly helps one get out of their "me place." By standing in someone else's proverbial shoes, not only might we see more clearly another's perspective, and perhaps feel more of what they might feel, but things might shift from seeming like it's all about us. Studies of virtuous leadership include compassion as one of five key values contributing to organizational virtuousness and performance. Not surprisingly, virtuous behaviors produce positive emotions in people, which help breed more virtuous behavior and greater positive well-being, building cumulatively. Employees' positive emotions lead to positive actions for the organization. Consider the earlier example of the leader who publicly offered compassion when an employee suffered a fatal heart attack.

Focus on what's going well and what is possible. Catch people doing things right. The practice of appreciative inquiry focuses on what is working and what could be. Even our language matters; positive words induce positive thinking and positive emotions. Ask more; dictate less. Celebrate successes—even incremental wins within a larger project—and learn from them.

Appreciate people. Recognize employees for good work; show sincere appreciation with your words and with small gifts or perks. These actions can be public or private, and they go a long way to extend people's energy and help them to feel valued—thereby fueling positive emotions and continued productivity. A simple heartfelt "thank you" pays significant dividends, especially relative to the effort it takes. Remember to treat mistakes as sources of information from which individuals learn, and to encourage people to explore alternate ways to solve problems and achieve their goals.

Other ways to incorporate gratitude include encouraging the use of keeping gratitude journals, writing long-overdue letters of thanks, sending cards of appreciation and encouragement, and utilizing public white boards for open message sharing.

Allow employees to craft a portion of their jobs, exercise more autonomy with their work and how it's accomplished, and utilize their strengths. Job crafting is shown to enhance employees' meaningfulness, satisfaction, and thriving. A person's interests determine how strengths manifest. Studies by Gallup show that organizations with employees who use their strengths have 1.5 times the productivity of other organizations.

Simply identifying strengths appears to have benefits like increased happiness. Also, providing employees feedback about strengths instead of weaknesses results in greater engagement and productivity.

Establish or review workplace wellness programs to promote overall well-being. Research shows positive emotions improve coping, build resilience, and predict additional positive emotions, effectively creating an upward spiral with increasingly improved functioning and well-being. This poses a wonderful opportunity for people to take what actions they need to regularly experience positive emotion and grow to their optimal well-being. Businesses can educate employees about this and propose relevant programs.

Consider opportunities for employees to refuel and restore. Numerous companies now provide meditation spaces, mindfulness programs, and other means for encouraging employees to slow down, reflect, and recharge. The positive impact on employees does have an effect on the bottom line.

Employ a practice known as *priming* to direct communication towards positive emotions. For example, begin and end meetings on a positive note. Research shows that mental acuity is greater when one simply imagines positive (versus negative) events—so put a good thought in their heads first. Ask someone to share a story about something for which she is extremely grateful, or about the best thing that happened in the week, thereby incorporating elevation.

Create opportunities for social interaction and developing meaningful relationships, both in and outside the work environment. Brainstorm how employees can create positive working relationships. There is an entire body of work on the impact of positive relationships in the workplace, illustrating their link to positive emotions and emphasizing the benefits to organizations. Consider offering communal spaces and activities that bring employees together. For example, establish options for working together on community projects. There is also evidence suggesting behaviors and emotions spread unconsciously through social networks (it's called *social contagion*).

Smile. It sounds simple; it is. The impact is significant. For as long as memory serves me, I've had a habit of smiling at people, including strangers and passers-by. Perhaps it is a learned behavior from my extroverted and optimistic dad. I'm not sure, but the effect is that people generally smile back—not always, but usually—which feels like a gift in return, with both people coming away with more. It's not that I'm constantly in a good mood and walking around with a smiley face; I have bad moments and bad days like anyone. It does make a difference, though, in terms of the general reception from others. The energy is contagious.

Cultivating positivity is not simply about acting happy, and it's certainly not about denying reality. It means working toward empirically-proven methods for improving one's well-being—and in a way that impacts an organization's bottom line, too. Martin Seligman coined the term "learned optimism" to explain his research findings, that optimism can be developed and enhanced through interventions.

Numerous studies exist to support the application of positive psychology for helping individuals and organizations thrive. Research shows that positive emotions have lasting effects for the organization. Positivity helps make employees and managers more effective not only in the moment of experiencing the positive emotion, but also for long-term success. This is good news for any enterprise and offers a basis for incorporating programs, techniques, and tools for applying these principles and practices to greater effectiveness in the workplace.

Positive emotional states strengthen intellectual, physical, and social abilities, plus the full range of one's combined psychological resources. Because organizations are comprised of people, the well-being of those people matters. Cameron's work showed that a company's high scores in positive practices improved both employee and customer retention, plus six measures of financial performance.

It's a choice. The client I mentioned earlier, who was prepared to quit her job out of desperation and frustration—she made a choice. She decided it was not feasible to leave her company before landing a new position, yet she wanted to feel better about being there every day. Dwelling on her misery was not serving her well. Making it a point to notice what she appreciated, and staying hopeful about potential new opportunities, her outlook improved—as did her job prospects.

Small changes can always produce significant results, especially if those small changes are meaningful. A practice of positivity can make a meaningful change for any person, and for any organization too.

Cheryl Schofield

Cheryl Schofield is a professional coach and consultant with extensive experience helping organizations and individuals improve and grow.

Cheryl supports and helps empower people seeking clarity, direction, and development in their careers and their lives, focusing on their strengths and what's possible. She brings a combination of energy, respect, empathy and authenticity to the client relationship— emphasizing goals, action and results. She assists organizations and individuals in achieving targets through her breadth and depth of experience with human capital matters.

As a human resources leader supporting numerous lines of business in a multi-billion -dollar organization, Cheryl was instrumental in contributing to the success of the company and its talented employees through a positive focus and dedicated investment in human potential, coaching, and development. Her clients are with businesses and non-profit organizations to include Advance Auto, Northern Trust, Walgreens, Whirlpool, and United Airlines.

Cheryl holds a Master of Education degree with an emphasis in positive coaching and a graduate certificate in positive psychology, both from the University of Missouri-Columbia. She received her Bachelor's degree in psychology from Northern Illinois University, and coach training from Coach University, Inc. Cheryl is a member of the International Coach Federation, as well as the Institute of Coaching at McClean Hospital, and the International Positive Psychology Association.

Additionally, Cheryl has a keen interest in integrative wellness and therapeutic healing arts, and is a board-certified clinical hypnosis practitioner with medical support specialization.

Cheryl resides in the Chicago area. You can contact her at coach@cherylschofield.com or 815-861-3733.

Leslie S. Schreiber

How Sticky Notes and "Thinking Hats"
Can Save a Culture

"Open your eyes!" I told them.

The group of 20 healthcare employees opened their eyes and began to buzz again with conversation.

"Let me see yours!"

"Wow, look at that!"

Gary was especially excited. With his tough exterior, he was the usually the critical curmudgeon of the group (the one who was less afraid to be honest since he'd held his job for many years). "I just can't believe that they all turned out so different," he exclaimed. "I mean, look at Jerry's. It's like he heard a completely different set of directions!" Jerry's snowflake had three distinct holes while Gary's didn't have any.

Everyone in the group was holding up their own piece of white paper which now resembled some sort of snowflake. Moments before, I had instructed them to tear off the upper right corner, fold the paper in half, tear off the lower left corner, fold in half again, and so on—but with their eyes closed the whole time, and in silence.

"What do you make of this, Gary?" I asked.

"It's a great reminder that we can have different interpretations and therefore different perspectives," he said. He went on to talk about how important it seemed to honor those differences and how hard that can be when the company culture doesn't encourage new ideas, openness, and creativity.

I was impressed—Gary had hit the nail on the head for me, and he became one of my most attentive students during our Six Thinking Hats training.

Why Six Thinking Hats?

Over the past 15 years, I have had the privilege of being invited into more than 25 different companies, non-profits, and government organizations. My work with them has focused on creating healthy cultures by strengthening and improving employee relationships. This includes people in both leadership and non-leadership positions, board members as well as volunteers.

As my business has grown, I have become intrigued by innovation and creativity in the workplace. How can a culture foster these important qualities and encourage the best ideas from people, but still maintain positive relationships between all of the employees?

So I began asking my clients:

- How does your workplace value differing ideas?
- How often are they sought out?
- How easily do employees consider perspectives different from their own?
- How is conflict handled?

As many consultants know, the answers I received did not always match the reality of the workplace. So I asked permission to sit in on my clients' meetings. I would be observing the following criteria:

- Is there structure? Or is it informal?
- Is there room for debate? Or is there fear of conflict?
- Are new ideas and creativity welcomed? Or is preserving the status quo most important?
- Is everyone involved? Or just the vocal few?
- Are assumptions questioned? Or is faulty information taken as fact?
- Are decisions thoroughly examined? Or are risk factors overlooked?

With these questions, I could ascertain not only the effectiveness of their meetings, but also a great deal about the company culture. Does the culture value open and honest discussion? Is there an expectation to be innovative and creative while solving problems? How do people convey respect? Do people feel a sense of teamwork?

Around this time, I was introduced to Edward deBono's *Six Thinking Hats*. I read a lot of testimony about the effectiveness of this approach, and I repeat two such selections here because I would willingly say the same:

> "The Hats helped us overcome cultural differences—interdepartmental, cultural, and international differences—as everyone uses a common language in meetings. It contributes to build effective teams and enhances their performance. It also facilitates the transfer of ideas, technologies and systems from one part of an organization to another."

> "The methods helped us promote positive relationships, reduce the frustrations normally felt in meetings and the deterioration in personal relationships caused by adversarial debate. People leave meetings in a positive frame of mind. Its use will therefore contribute to a much more positive, cooperative and constructive climate, which will reduce negative stress." *

The premise to this novel approach was that *recognizing and understanding the role of thinking* was critical to a company's culture. Six Thinking Hats introduced the concepts of Traditional Thinking, Parallel Thinking, and Lateral Thinking. It encouraged the use of emotional thoughts and playful ideas. And as a practical bonus, it claimed that it could reduce meeting time by up to 50 percent!

My degree in Philosophy helped me embrace this concept of "thinking as critical to culture," but I wasn't fully sold until I experienced the Six Hats process. Then I saw its value immediately, particularly when leading meetings where creative thinking was needed to move beyond a particular mindset.

What is **Six Thinking Hats?**

Six Thinking Hats® is a meeting management tool that harnesses parallel thinking as well as individual process time, group brainstorming, and application of action items. Developed by Edward deBono, M.D. in 1985, over 700,000 people have been trained and implemented this model that is based on differentiating between six distinct colors of hats that are metaphors for six different 'ways of thinking':

WHITE HAT	Neutral, objective thinking, concerned with facts
RED HAT	Emotional, intuitive thinking
BLACK HAT	Skeptical, negative, critical thinking
YELLOW HAT	Sunny, positive, optimistic thinking
GREEN HAT	Creative, innovative thinking
BLUE HAT	Cool, organized, summarized thinking

So, how does it work? Let's envision a traditional two-hour meeting. This meeting involves the following typical characters: the optimistic sales manager, the creative marketing manager, the fact-driven finance manager, a critical-curmudgeon operations manager, (just think "I've been working here for 20 years and I know why that won't work"), and their impulsive supervisor (who will arrive late to the meeting).

Let's imagine they have come together to discuss how to improve the time it takes to deliver online orders. The marketing manager begins to present an idea. The sales manager is already on board with him—but it turns south from here. The finance manager wants to know the data supporting the idea and begins to question the marketing manager for it. The curmudgeonly operations manager points out everything that won't work about the idea. The marketing manager becomes defensive and the sales manager says she still thinks it's a good idea.

If you imagine this going on for 2 hours, you can imagine it repeating itself quite a bit. An example like this has typical indications of Traditional Thinking, which is when argument and proving the other wrong dominate the discussion. By the way, the supervisor arrives at this point, senses the growing conflict in the room, and quickly decides to table the topic for another meeting.

A Typical Six Hats Meeting

If this were a Six Thinking Hats meeting, Parallel Thinking would be used instead of Traditional Thinking. Parallel Thinking is when everyone thinks in the same way at the same time. In other words, everyone wears the same "hat" concurrently.

For example, a Process Improvement agenda could look something like this:

FOCUS: We need to reduce our time from order to delivery.
OUTCOME: At least five new ideas to help us reduce our time from order to delivery.
TOTAL TIME: 60 minutes

WHITE HAT	Review the current process. (5 minutes)
YELLOW HAT	What's working well with the process? (10 minutes)
BLACK HAT	What are the weaknesses in the process? (10 minutes)
GREEN HAT	Generate ideas to overcome the weaknesses. (25 minutes)
RED HAT	Choose the best five ideas. (3 minutes)
BLUE HAT	What do we need to do, by when? (7 minutes)

An important tenet of Six Thinking Hats is that the success of any discussion depends upon participation. Everyone participates equally in this meeting because the first 1-2 minutes "wearing" each hat is spent individually and silently writing down responses on 3X5 sticky notes. Each idea you're writing down is given its own sticky note. This ensures that no idea is lost and that all ideas are encouraged.

Next, we take turns sharing one idea per person. If someone has a similar idea, they simply discard their sticky note (no need to repeat an idea if there's nothing to add). The go-round continues until all of the sticky notes have been read. This simple process reinforces the concept of group work and reduces time spent on repetitive contributions.

During reporting, the sticky notes are posted on flip charts, the wall, or somewhere visible—and will remain visible the entire meeting. In nearly every Six Thinking Hats training I have conducted, I have heard someone appreciatively say, "What a great idea!" or "I would have never thought of that."

As the agenda is followed, everyone's preference in how they think is met. Yet they are also encouraged to stretch themselves by thinking in a different way. The naturally optimistic sales manager will have to contribute in Black Hat (critical) ways, and the critical curmudgeon will have to take their turn contributing in Yellow Hat (positive) ways as well.

Using this approach, many meetings that typically run two hours have been cut in half, reduced to only one hour. At the end of that hour, five new and thoroughly-examined ideas are ready for action. Each person participated and had an opportunity to use their strengths. Plus, the rest of the information from the meeting was captured on sticky notes. Finally, as with many tools, Six Thinking Hats becomes easier and quicker to use the more familiar people are with it.

Instead of falling into typical conflicts caused by people's differing agendas and personality types, time is spent pooling ideas rather than attacking or getting defensive over them. By thinking in parallel, you save time, you save money, everyone stays engaged in the process, and the whole team generates more (and better) ideas.

When Is It Appropriate to Use Six Thinking Hats?
Many clients ask if it's appropriate to use this methodology for every meeting. A straight-forward status-update meeting, for instance, may not benefit from the Six Thinking Hats approach. Use your own discretion.

There are many meeting topics, however, that lend themselves especially well to Six Thinking Hats methodology. These include any subject around Strategic Planning, Process Improvement, Problem Solving, Exploration, Idea Generation, and Evaluation.

The following factors will help determine if using Six Thinking Hats is a good fit for a particular meeting:

1. When those attending have strongly held and different views.
2. When there is rambling discussion that is not getting anywhere.
3. When a subject needs to be examined thoroughly.
4. When a decision has to be made while looking at a number of different perspectives.
5. When creative thinking is needed to move beyond a particular mindset.
6. When an evaluation of a topic or person is being given, such as a performance review.

As one client recently wrote to me in an email, she now uses Six Thinking Hats as a filter for any type of meeting. She wrote me: "This model changed the way I do my work. I have lots of meetings to acquire the needs and knowledge of the business units. And even if they don't know the Six Hats model, I can still apply it just using different words."

When Else Can You Use Six Hats?
You can also apply parallel thinking to individual thinking, the way people might write a pros (yellow hat) and cons (black hat) list for themselves. But with Six Hats, there are the added perspectives of examining the facts (white hat), listening to your intuition (red hat), and allowing yourself to think creatively (green hat).

I'll often encourage clients to incorporate Six Thinking Hats into their company language. For example, the terminology can be useful beyond the meetings themselves, as when you discuss topics via email. "I'd like to know your White Hat thoughts on this proposal." Or, "Is there too much Red Hat thinking going on in this decision?" Or, "Off the top of your head, what are three Green Hat ideas to counter this problem?"

So when you next find yourself at work and wanting to say to that critical curmudgeon don't be so negative, why not say instead, "What's your yellow-hat thinking on that?"

Take-Aways

Having been a Six Hats facilitator and trainer for over 7 years, I can testify to the importance of diverse thinking in healthy organizational cultures. Six Thinking Hats encourages this diversity in a systematic way, which enables employees to do the following during meetings:

- Take on different perspectives
- Reduce conflict
- Increase a sense of team
- Increase appreciation for others' ideas
- Increase energy
- Increase clarity
- Increase innovation

And as Gary discovered through his snowflake, appreciating different modes of thinking is valuable. Six Hats makes that easy to do.

Good thinking to you!

* For case studies, please read Innovation: Case by Case by Barbara Stennes, published by deBono Thinking Systems, 2004.

Leslie S. Schreiber

M.Ed.

White Hat: Facts About Leslie S. Schreiber, M. Ed. —
Georgetown University, Organizational Consulting and Change Leadership certificate
George Mason University, Leadership Coaching for Organizational Well-Being certificate
Saint Michael's College, Masters in Experiential Education
Mary Washington University, B.A. in Philosophy

Yellow Hat: Positive thinking about Leslie—She is known for having an optimistic outlook on things and people. Her welcoming, relaxed style of training, facilitation, and coaching make her well liked. She is entering the 15th year of owning her own consulting and training business!

Black Hat: Critical thinking about Leslie—she dislikes spicy food. (That's negative, right?)

Green Hat: Innovative thinking about Leslie—she is in the process of receiving a certificate in Human Centered Design Thinking!

Red Hat: Intuitive thinking about Leslie—passionate about her work! Excellent communicator! Community builder! Provides great energy!

Blue Hat: Summarized thinking about Leslie—contact Leslie ASAP to help with meetings and culture!

EMAIL leslie@schreibertraining.com
PHONE 802-324-8326
LINKEDIN /in/leslieschreiberleadership

Cynthia M. Schuler

Follow the Leader:
A Roadmap for Cultivating and Maintaining
a Positive Organizational Culture

I think we've all worked in an organization where a negative culture exists. Colleagues and subordinates don't have anything nice to say about the organization; there is no real teamwork; employees do not smile and laugh with each other; no one shows pride in the organization, or confidence in what they are producing. When you walk the halls, there is a sense that employees just don't want to be there. On the flip side, I am sure that most of us have also been employed with an organization where the mood is upbeat—where top executives, managers, and subordinates smile and say hello when they pass each other in the hallway, where everyone is working together to help the organization reach success.

I am convinced, after many years in the field of Human Resources, that culture must be taught from the top down and lived every day in the life of an organization in order for that organization to be successful. A positive culture can't be cultivated and maintained unless the leaders of an organization take the time to understand and digest the purpose of an organization, unless those leaders genuinely believe in the purpose of the organization, and unless those leaders live the culture by displaying behavior that supports it on a daily basis.

As Merriam-Webster's simple definition states, *culture* is "the beliefs, customs, arts, etc. of a particular society, group, place or time," or "a way of thinking, behaving, or working that exists in a place or organization (such as a business)." An additional definition is "the set of shared values, attitudes, goals and practices that characterize an institution or organization (such as a business). With these definitions of culture squarely in mind, I challenge all leaders of organizations to think about how they'd answer the questions below:

1. Do you know your organization's vision and mission?
2. Do you truly believe in the purpose of the organization?
3. Do you understand your role in the organization?
4. Now, how would you describe the culture of your organization?

5. Do you play an active role in cultivating the culture of the organization by believing in it openly and displaying the behavior that it calls for?
6. Do your colleagues and subordinates follow your lead?

Defining an Organization

We can't begin to cultivate any type of culture in an organization unless some basic issues have been discussed and resolved when the organization is created. These issues can be documented in a written strategic plan, or they can be discussed and agreed upon verbally by the founders of an organization. When defining the culture of an organization, consider the following:

1. What is the industry in which you operate?
2. What the vision and mission of the organization?
3. Who are the clients of the organization?
4. What will set the organization apart from other organizations?
5. What do you want to convey to internal and external clients about the organization?

Once you've discussed and agreed upon these factors, you should then focus on attracting leaders who believe in the vision and mission of the organization. As we know, behavior is learned. If we, as leaders, are able to attract colleagues and subordinates who share our sentiments about the organizations we love and cherish, it should be fairly easy to attract and lead others naturally. This, in turn, will impact the bottom-line success of the organization.

In "Why People Follow the Leader" in *Harvard Business Review* in September of 2004, Michael Maccoby writes that leaders attract followers, and followers respond to a leader's attitude. Behavior is emulated. Think about it: when you smile and say hello to someone, generally they will smile and say hello in return. When you offer a helping hand to others, generally they will offer a helping hand to someone else (or think about it more). When cultivating a *positive* organizational culture, it is imperative to employ leaders who are able to attract followers who will emulate their behavior—which is the right behavior.

Cultivating a Positive Organizational Culture

Once the vision and mission of an organization is defined and leaders are recruited to carry out the organization's mission, it is time to begin to cultivate a positive organizational culture. While reality is that leaders may not be successful in cultivating and transferring a positive organizational culture for all colleagues and subordinates, it is essential for leaders to put their best effort forth and lead by example. Below are ten very simple tips on beginning to cultivate a positive culture:

1. Create an environment of diversity and inclusion. Leaders must make employees feel welcome and comfortable during the onboarding process (from the offer letter stage through the physical arrival of the employee at the organization – then throughout the employee's tenure with the organization). During the onboarding process, make certain all employees spend time with a leader in the organization in an effort to understand the vision and mission of the organization. In addition, it's important that each employee know and understand how his or her role will contribute to the bottom-line success of the organization. Take an interest in each employee and make an effort to get to know their interests, strengths, and weaknesses. Understand that each employee has had unique experiences that have shaped him or her, and look to learn and appreciate those differences.

As a second part of this, consider the workspace design. Is it comfortable? Does it allow for employees to interact and share ideas? Do cubicles work here, or is there a better design where employees could interact differently and more effectively? Is the area dark or is there sufficient light so that employees feel energized and ready to contribute? If the department is in an enclosed area, are employees encouraged to brainstorm important initiatives and projects in other spaces where they may feel more comfortable and free to share ideas?

2. Empower subordinates. All employees must have a voice. Conduct departmental meetings and encourage participation and sharing ideas, especially while all employees are present. Each employee has something to contribute. Leaders must also allow employees to speak up at meetings and challenge each other respectfully. Agree to disagree. Conduct brainstorming sessions. Accept all ideas as creative solutions even if all of the ideas presented are not implemented.

3. Develop an open door policy . . . and mean it. Leaders should adopt an open-door policy and communicate that a knock is all that is needed if their door is closed. As leaders, we must remember that continuous communication is imperative in cultivating a positive culture. Make time to meet with employees, walk around and talk to employees, and listen to what employees have to say. Developing and implementing an open-door policy will assist in building a mutual trust. Trust and respect are earned; this is one way to earn them gradually. And remember that open door means open door. How many times have you had the door closed when an employee knocked on the door in "crisis mode"? What if they really needed you and thought you were truly unavailable? It is important to remember that our human capital is critical to the success of our organizations; therefore we, as leaders, must make ourselves available to those who are looking to us to guide them.

4. Be vulnerable. No one is perfect. Admit when you make a mistake, or when a colleague or subordinate offers a more efficient way to accomplish a task. Confident leaders do not need to take credit for other's ideas. Be proud of your colleagues and subordinates and give credit for an idea or implementation where it's due.

5. Promote teamwork. Encourage your team to work together to come up with ideas and solutions to problems. Remember: in an inclusive environment, everyone has different skills, and ALL skills are needed to be maximally successful. The work of a team is far more powerful than the work of a single individual.

6. Mentor and coach. Take mentoring and coaching seriously. In other words: *take an interest in all employees.* Get to know each person and take an interest in their professional growth and short- and long-term goals. Accept each person for his/her personal and professional background and look to capitalize on at least one strength of each employee. Meet with subordinates quarterly to discuss goal development and progress. Offer advice on how to approach challenging situations with other colleagues. Coach employees with respect to their professional goals. What are their personal goals? Is this position just a stepping stone? Are there other opportunities in the organization for which the employee can be coached and grown? Coaching is essential—even if it means coaching someone up and out of the organization to pursue other interests.

7. Be honest and loyal. Leaders must display honesty and loyalty. Everyone must be treated equally across the board. If subordinates see that you "talk the talk" and "walk the walk," a trust and respect will develop naturally and the employee will likely be loyal and committed to being productive for you and for the organization. In Marla Tabaka's "10 Behaviors to Cultivate a Powerful Culture," she repeats an idea from author Nan

Russell: that "people don't give their ideas, discretionary efforts, enthusiasm, or best work to people they don't trust."

8. Display a good work ethic. Arrive at work on time, and let your subordinates know when you will be late, out of the office, or leaving early. Work hard and show a mutual respect for all employees. Show employees that while you may be called a "supervisor," "manager," "director," or some other title, you are still colleagues. Never refer to a subordinate as "someone who works for me." Treating a subordinate as a colleague will be recognized and respected by that person.

9. Praise good work. A simple "thank you" means more to colleagues and subordinates than leaders understand. Recognizing an employee or colleague for their hard work (especially when it helps you) has a profound effect. Conversely, moving mountains and putting in 150% effort every day and rarely hearing that same simple "thank you" may affect a colleague or a subordinate in a negative way.

10. Smile. A smile sets the tone for your employees for the entire work day. We have all had to deal with personal issues in the evening after work, or in the morning before work. Traffic in a major metropolitan area can also contribute negatively to a morning mood—a lot of us know. In general, body language speaks volumes! So do your best to leave the personal issues at the door; the team looks to that leader the moment he or she walks in that door. Say "hello" and "good morning" to everyone and start the day on a positive note. First impressions always count.

There are many other things leaders can do to cultivate a positive culture. The ten tips above are just a few tips to get started. While it can be overwhelming, most of the tips stated above are natural behaviors; when we display these behaviors and earn the trust and respect of our colleagues and employees, the same behaviors will be emulated and will shape the culture of the organization.

Maintaining a Positive Organizational Culture

We have now seen how positive organizational cultures are defined and cultivated. The final piece to the puzzle is how to maintain that positive culture and to measure whether or not the culture has changed—and if so, why it has changed.

First things first: if you have negativity at the top of an organization, realize that your most important people—the leaders who are trying to influence subordinates and colleagues across the organization—will have a very difficult time imposing a positive culture on colleagues and subordinates and may eventually become unhappy themselves. Unfortunately, it is hard to hide unhappiness. Second: if leaders are negative, the behaviors they display will be negative, and employees will pick up on those behaviors and emulate them. The chain reaction will then begin in the same way, which could ultimately result in a (more) toxic and negative organizational culture.

Executives must also take an interest in the other people who are leading their organizations and nurture them as they are nurturing others. While organizations look to leaders to make a lasting impact on organizations, don't forget that leaders need encouragement too. Transparency, continuous communication, and showing leaders they are valued is essential too.

Lastly: how do we measure change in organizational culture? Engagement surveys, mid-year reviews, stay interviews, 360-degree reviews, and metrics on turnover and exit interviews will assist in measuring the positivity or negativity of an organization's culture. While it is time-consuming and sometimes difficult to convince employees that their answers to engagement surveys are anonymous, it is important and cost-effective if organizations actually use the information they gather to affect change as needed.

It is not guaranteed that leaders will be able to influence all colleagues and subordinates while cultivating a positive culture in an organization. But I remain convinced that I can guarantee this: if we, as leaders, truly believe in the purpose of an organization, and if we lead by example and follow some simple advice by way of the tips offered earlier, we should not have difficulty attracting others who will observe us and emulate the behavior they witness. In leading by example, we are more likely to influence others to follow our lead in helping cultivate the culture we want for the organizations we love. And ultimately, if we keep the lines of communication open and continuously display behavior that will be emulated by others, we will likely be able to maintain that positive culture which will, in turn, assist in the bottom line success of our organizations.

As Matt Rizai, CEO, Workiva states in "4 Ways to Build a Workplace Culture That Empowers People":

> "One of the biggest indicators of a vibrant workplace culture is the willingness of a company to place more value on its people than on process . . . In the people economy, employees aren't viewed merely as headcount, but rather as the engine that spurs innovation, drives market growth, satisfies customers, and builds brand value."

The bottom line is that an organization's success is dependent on happy human capital who trust and believe in an organization, and who are willing to work hard to help the organization achieve its success. If we recruit leaders into our organizations who truly believe in the purpose of organization and live the purpose, who walk the walk and talk the talk, that's what others will begin to do—and in ways not seen before, the colleagues and subordinates around them will begin to produce results that mean a bigger change to the bottom line that anyone knew to expect from mutual trust and respect.

ABOUT THE AUTHOR

Cynthia M. Schuler

PHR, SHRM-CP, CPRW

Cynthia M. Schuler is a 20-year veteran in the field of Human Resources and is currently Chief Human Resources Officer for an established law firm.

Cynthia has been working in law firms for nearly 30 years, beginning her tenure in HR as an HR Assistant and working her way up to Chief Human Resources Officer. She has seen the transformation in HR from paper-pushing to pushing the envelope for business and wielding "people power" in new and valuable ways.

Cynthia manages the full cycle of human resources including talent management, benefits and compensation, employee relations, and professional development and training. She holds a Master's Degree in Business Administration and a Professional in Human Resources Certification (PHR). She is also a Society of Human Resources Certified Personal (SHRM-CP) and a Certified Professional Resume Writer (CPRW).

Cynthia has published numerous articles and conducted presentations for multiple organizations including Society for Human Resources Japan INSIGHTS magazine, National Business Institute, Business and Legal Reports, and the American Management Association.

EMAIL cmschuler@msn.com
LINKEDIN /in/cindys1

Ken Silay

Innovation Depends on a Culture That Thinks

Innovation—every business knows its importance, and every business works hard to weave it into their advertising and slogans. But when you begin to dig deeper into an organization, does innovation actually dive deeper into the substance of the company than the marketing department?

Innovation has been a constant theme through multiple management philosophies over the past thirty to forty years. From In Search of Excellence by Peters and Waterman in the eighties through Forbes Magazine's identification of the Innovation Premium in the 2010s, cultivating and nurturing the creative spark in an organization has always been a key focus of management philosophy. Innovation requires the ability to think differently and the guts to budget money and time with the belief that the organization's future depends upon it. It requires that people step away from day-to-day operations, as today will always take precedence over tomorrow.

Most companies don't have the stomach for genuine innovation. They won't or can't stay the course. In their case, innovation is just a great word to include in the quarterly financial results and the annual report.

People are surprised innovation isn't a brainstorming session. It's not a group of executives sitting in a room dreaming up great new ideas. It's not someone else's job. It's an organization mindset, and one that few companies come by naturally. Most people in most organizations are focused on the day-to-day given the necessity of achieving quarterly results; that naturally creates tunnel vision and short-term thinking. Focusing only on the present is a guarantee that you will always remain there.

Let me illustrate with a quick story.

People who trap animals in Africa for zoos in America say that one of the hardest animals to catch is the ring-tailed monkey. For the Zulus native to that continent, however, it's simple. They've been catching this agile little animal with ease as long as we've paid attention. The method the Zulus use is based on knowledge of the animal; their trap is nothing more than a melon growing on a vine. The ring-tailed monkey loves the seeds of this melon, so the Zulus simply cut a hole in the melon just large enough for the monkey to insert his hand to reach the seeds inside. The monkey will stick his hand in, grab as many seeds as he can, then start to pull it out. But he can't—because, with a fist full of seeds, its hand is now larger than the hole. The monkey will pull and tug, screech, and fight the melon for hours. But the only way for a monkey to free itself of the melon is to give up the seeds, which it won't. After the monkey is stuck, the Zulus need only sneak up and grab him. By holding on to what he has right now, he loses everything.

Often you hear phrases like *we need to go back to what made us successful.* That's the battle cry of a dying corporate culture. In football, if you retreat backwards into your own end zone and get caught, it's called a *safety*—and the other team earns points for that. There is nothing safe about an organization getting caught in the past. Organizations that "go back to their roots" as a default when times get challenging are guaranteeing that they will end up there again sometime in the future.

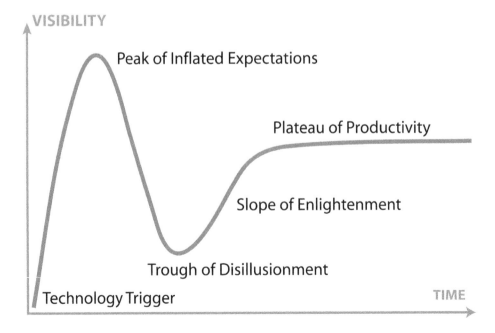

Gartner, a well-known information technology research and advisory company, utilizes a methodology called the Hype Cycle (shown on the previous page) which provides a graphical view of the maturity, adoption, and business application of specific technologies. If I plotted innovation on a hype cycle today, I might believe organizations are moving into a *trough of disillusionment*—the point at which interest wanes as experiments and implementations fail to deliver. But I might also believe that it would begin to ascend the slope of enlightenment—the next phase of the Hype Cycle, where more benefits of the innovation can visibly crystallize for the organization and become more widely understood. Then, if an innovation is to survive, it has to become part of the culture.

As I've mentioned, people seem to use the word innovation just for its connotation, or to be trendy. If you ask 10 people to define innovation, you will likely get 10 different answers. This is my definition of innovation: the collective wisdom of a forward-thinking organization, distilled from motivated people who execute a defined process capable of outmatching their competitiondelivering unmatched achievements.

Let's talk about collective wisdom. Wisdom is insight, or the ability to see beyond the surface of an issue or problem. Some people can do that naturally, but for others, it must be learned. It's important for any organization expecting innovation to foster a culture that encourages an individual's ability to think beyond the status quo—to question whether one plus one really equals two. If someone doesn't know what that means, remind them that most great ideas are not the product of a single mind, but are small notions refined by each person they touch, until they reach the person who can finally put them together with permanence. Bringing people together to share different—even conflicting— insights helps the organization to reach the best outcome that yields some collective wisdom.

Since we already discussed the need for an organization to be forward-thinking (remember the monkey?), why do individuals need motivation and fortitude? It's hard to stay focused on innovating when, for instance, the network is down and thousands of salespeople can't process transactions for customers. But innovation isn't all new inventions—and it's not just for companies that are succeeding today. If we don't continually innovate to prepare for tomorrow, we risk the long-term survival of our companies. It takes effort, persistence, and maybe some extra time to find breakthrough ideas—and even then, truly novel ideas are most often met with skepticism and criticism. This is why it takes some strength of conviction—and not just imagination—to see innovation all the way through.

Innovation requires a combination of "blue sky" and structure to develop a well-thought out plan that fits culture but also has a process to adapt—as technology and business both change over time. This is the paradox that surrounds the successful integration of innovation into an organization's culture: a free-flowing process that enables innovative thinking, but with it, the structure required to make the process successful. And you do need both.

There is a notion that innovation takes the form of a quarterly brainstorming session, and this session is supposed to yield all the ideas an organization needs. Obviously, this is simplistic thinking. Therefore, while it's no small challenge, I believe that innovation starts with changing the way that people think. While innovation can take the form of a product or app—a single, focused invention—focusing those energies into a single product is a recipe for one-and-done innovation, the kind that doesn't last.

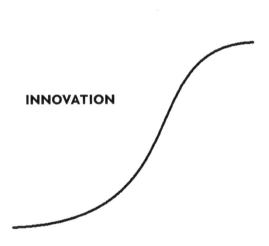

If an organization is to sustain its own innovation, it must build a culture that follows an ongoing series of S-curves, or waves of innovation. Each potential emerging technology follows this curve (shown above).

As with all technology, there is a life cycle for each innovation. Each idea or innovation typically follows this S-curve which shows its performance over time; it begins with a relatively flat initiation (or exploration) stage as it finds its place in the market. As the innovation emerges or is recognized within the marketplace, the curve steepens and the performance takes off; revenues increase and marketing is ramped up. All innovations, whether technology-inspired or not, eventually reach a maturity in the market and are either improved to extend that maturity or slowly retired or replaced. Nonetheless, the performance curve begins to level off.

Ideally, the innovation process within the organization is incubating multiple ideas, and each has its own performance curve. One or more innovations should be starting as others emerge or reach maturity.

But this continuous wave of innovations will not continue to flow if the company lacks a culture that embraces innovation.

Innovation starts in a culture when that spark of wisdom is ignited in every individual—that spark which constantly challenges the current and prepares for the future—and when that spark can be shared, questioned, and enhanced by others. Enabling that collaborative thinking process is essential in the beginning. Creating a pipeline of ideas is key. Then, once the idea pipeline is working, there needs to be a structured process that consistently collects, evaluates, and promotes worthy ideas to prototype and potentially injects them into the strategic planning process. It's not supposed to stop with a suggestion box; it's truly a process of management that, when adopted, can allow people to believe they're truly contributing to the organization's success.

Let's talk more about the process that's needed to create a continuing wave of innovation for an organization. This process progresses from idea generation through idea evaluation to idea implementation.

Eventually, new technology or other types of innovative ideas will become part of the strategic plan. Innovation is the hard work that is accomplished before you enter the strategic planning process. Ideas should be evaluated against long-term corporate initiatives—the key future expectations that will support corporate vision and, essentially, create challenge for the competition.

Strong companies with a passion for the future will find a way to innovate. If you believe innovation is a luxury for your organization, the future will belong to some other organization that embraces it.

Change is inevitable, but growth is optional. The pace of technological change requires you to look forward to survive. Change is hard—but I would rather be the catalyst for change than the victim of it!

We know it's good to be innovative, and we certainly know it's attractive. What many don't expect is the level of commitment needed to engage in innovation's real work, or the level of risk to which anyone is subject in pursuit of innovation's rewards. Frankly, most business executives are not willing to make those commitments for any number of reasons, principally fear of failure. In a November 2015 interview, Geoffrey Moore, author of Crossing the Chasm and Escape Velocity, said that "sustaining innovation is the lifeblood of any enterprise . . . sustaining innovations are the key to consistent performance, whereas disruptive innovations are the key to dramatic changes to power."

Forbes Magazine identifies the world's 100 most innovative companies by a specific calculation: the innovation premium. This metric measures how much the company's current valuation exceeds the value implicit in its current business. Think about what investors do with stocks: why are they willing to pay more for a company's shares than the shares are currently worth? Because they are expecting new growth from that company; they are expecting new income streams to emerge in the future. And where does most growth come from? Primarily from launching new products or services or entering new markets—both of which maintain innovation as their primary challenge.

So if innovation—creating new products or entering new markets—generates future income, what keeps executives from making the decision to engage? Is it culture, a lack of talent, executive commitment, or potentially a belief system that blocks a sustainable innovation strategy? Is there any evidence to support what really drives innovation? The solution to any problem begins with identifying the root cause of the issue.

One source of information you should investigate is the World Database of Innovation maintained and updated by Innovators International (www.innovatorsinternational.com). It contains information gathered from over 2000+ organizations, and it suggests many proven practices for developing new products, new processes, new businesses, and new technology.

The Database's underlying research indicates that there are more than 105 discernible Innovation Management Structures, Belief Systems, Processes, Talent Management Practices, and Culture Practices. What's interesting is that the fastest-growing, most serial innovators held only 27 of those in common. These companies are repeatedly and reliably transforming their current markets, inventing entirely new markets to the world, owning these new markets, making repeated significant leaps in top line growth, and gaining market share. Repeatable, sustainable innovation is not an accident. Does your organization have the capability to innovate within its DNA? More importantly: can you be competitive without it? Along with integrity, accountability, and teamwork, initiative is a key trait for a leader. To be a leader in today's marketplace requires the initiative to not only plan tactically for the short term, but to innovate and thus remain competitive for the future.

An ancient philosopher once said that "the lucky person passes for a genius." I believe that luck is simply where preparation meets opportunity. You must prepare for the future, or you might not be ready when the opportunity of a lifetime presents itself. If an organization can ever expect to sustain innovation, it must develop a genius for innovation; one definition of genius is the ability to recognize the power of new combinations. It's not necessarily the implementation of a single idea; in today's world, it's how you combine technologies and processes to change, and not just meet, customer expectations.

Here's an example to illustrate the point. Ever heard of biomimicry? Biomimicry is the imitation of the models, systems, and elements of nature to solve complex human problems. We've used this way of thinking for inventions large and small; one large example would be Velcro, and at the smallest level (microscopic), we've managed to create genetically-engineered tools for delivering drugs to targeted places within the body. Joel Barker, noted futurist, author and lecturer, calls this "innovation at the verge"— the place where one thing and something completely different come together to trigger innovation. For another example, there's a beverage company who has partnered with a bottler and a communications organization to provide underserved South African communities with free Wi-Fi—by building it into soda vending machines.

But it is one thing to understand what innovation is—and quite another to build sustainable innovation. How does an organization know that it has the right stuff to develop and sustain a genius for innovation? That requires people who can sustain the effort—and a culture which sustains them.

Creating a thinking culture is essential to sustaining innovation in an organization—and thus, to sustaining the organization's success and survival. Make no mistake, factors like leadership and executive support and corporate funding are critical for innovative and inventive teams. But innovation fails where it does not belong to a corporate culture that welcomes it, that encourages each person to take a mental journey somewhere they've never been before. It's best if everyone can take that journey and come back better for it.

Ken Silay

Ken Silay is a thought leader on innovation in Retail and IT. He's an information technologist who can see the big picture—who focuses on getting organizations to think beyond the next quarter's results. He's contributed to this anthology because continued innovation is so important for sustainable growth, and he wants to give organizations a reason *and* methodology for engaging with innovation.

Ken has been responsible for directing cultural shifts towards innovation. In his role, he helps provide a strategic vision for companies, as well as direction on tactics and implementation. He helps companies generate new ideas, then review and incorporate them into their corporate strategies.

Ken's research and evaluation of emerging trends in IT helps determine the real value of certain innovations to an organization. To date, Ken has researched emerging trends such as 3D printing, wearable technology, Internet of Things, nanotechnology, and artificial intelligence (AI) in application to real organizations in real time. Ken has continued to support the technology needs of executive team members by publishing a newsletter to introduce emerging opportunities in technology and describe market trends that are beginning to drive positive disruptive change.

Aside from forward-looking technological changes, Ken has provided continuing leadership for the expansion of company RFID implementation across brands—even achieving consistent 95% inventory accuracy during his oversight.

Ken is a retired US Air Force Squadron Commander.

If you want to create an innovation culture that fuels sustainable growth for companies, contact Ken for more information.

EMAIL kensilay@gmail.com
WEBSITE www.kensilay.com
LINKEDIN /in/ken-silay-innovation-management-leader-92b3984

April L. Taylor

People, Not Personalities:
Building an Authentic Working Culture

It has always puzzled me when people ask: "How would you describe your culture?"

Every company has a standard "elevator speech" for their organization, its culture, and what it stands for—but that doesn't mean much until you put yourself in that culture.

To some extent, someone's personal values have to align with the company's values for a good fit. But there are other matters of fit that can adjust; sometimes a culture can change a person, or vice versa. Your own experiences and perspectives will shape how you respond to a culture.

Let me tell you about Maya. From the day she interviewed, Maya was a strong candidate. She asked about the company's culture during the interview. In response, her interviewer told her about the company's strong ethical foundation, the team's collaborative work style, the high level of personal connection with leadership, and the numerous opportunities for professional growth and development.

Sound like someplace you'd want to work? Maya thought so, too. She joined the organization, and in the days and weeks after she'd been hired, she found a lot of her interviewer's description to be accurate. She saw that employees would offer open and constructive feedback, that they were involved in one another's lives (or at least cared), and that they seemed to have a great deal to teach one another. This encouraged Maya to open up; given her subject matter expertise, she felt ready to contribute early on. Other team members sometimes seemed surprised by her willingness to speak up, but probably just because she was the "new kid on the block."

Over the next few weeks, the picture changed. Instead of being energized by work and encouraged by it, Maya felt exhausted by it. At first, she assumed it was just the newness of things, the role and routine she hadn't known before. But that wasn't it. As Maya stepped back, she realized that she was no longer open and flowing with ideas like she'd been in other companies. She started to remember the way her new co-workers would seem to bristle when she offered her opinion; over time, it seemed clearer that many of them dismissed Maya as a know-it-all. Maya decided, then, that the best way to fit in was to censor herself—to stay quiet. She became very intentional and short with her comments: the basics, and nothing more.

Eventually, Maya's manager noticed that she'd lost some of her energy. Maya was still a good employee—she met her goals—but she was clearly not "all in." There wasn't the same engagement, investment, and follow-through she'd promised and that she had delivered before. Maya was holding back, and at work she was wearing a mask: smiling, agreeable, but without sharing her truest and fullest thoughts.

When we discuss culture, we are discussing people. But there's a distinction between a person—the real heart, smarts, and soul of someone you hire—and personalities, which are the faces people wear in different places. (Sure enough, the Latin root of the word personality means mask.) We think of culture as though it's a blend of personalities, but really it's the intersection of people and their abilities.

On the subject of cultivating culture, here's my question: **how can an organization build a culture around authenticity—around people—and not around personalities?**

You could say, of Maya's workplace, that they did have "a good culture" in some ways. They were inviting the right kind of personalities. But they were not helping the people to connect, or to keep themselves open to new people. Maya entered that culture as an authentic and powerful person—but when aspects of her authenticity were punished instead of rewarded, she became less powerful as an employee. The culture, rather than encourage connection between her and others, compelled her to put on a "mask" and hide instead.

I believe that cultivating a great workplace culture requires the cultivation of authenticity. This chapter will discuss what we, as stewards of that workplace, can do to drive authentic thoughts and behaviors and lead teams to the best possible outcomes.

Let's start by talking a little about culture. We all know culture is dynamic; it changes. It's a moving target. It's easily swayed by the people within it—who might, in numerous ways, be in flux. Sometimes, single participants can make or break a culture (whether by coming or going).

We know, too, that culture has a tremendous impact on the bottom line of a business, whether it's clearly visible in certain places or not. The quality of an organization's culture has a lot to do with productivity, communication, and morale; it has a great impact on the engagement of each individual person and the cohesion of teams.

I'm not the first to say it, but a good culture should be grounded in values. Values are important even if the employees don't (yet) take them seriously. To validate this, just consider what happens when the leaders of an organization, or the organization as a whole, contradict the values; at those moments, the culture seems not to exist at all. This also illustrates how nearly any culture could benefit from honesty and consistency with those values.

This is where authenticity becomes an important practice for a healthy culture. *Authentic behavior*—people acting as they truly feel and intend, and not as they feel they "should"—means that people are naturally more honest because they feel free and open to be that way. Authenticity means that people can trust one another and avoid collecting into cliques, because they're just who they are, and they contribute in a meaningful way to the team. Authenticity means that people act on more permanent intentions: what they actually care about, and not just what seems most important at the time.

When people are forced to follow through as personalities—as people who wear a mask or "play a role" within a company—they are compelled by a need to fit in. They are compelled to maintain some kind of appearance, whether it's a meaningful appearance or not. Let me suggest: that's not the motive that drives employees at the best companies.

What authenticity, honesty, and most other virtues have in common is *choice*. A person chooses to be honest, or courageous, or compassionate—or authentic, true to themselves—or at least, they choose small acts that showcase those qualities. People who do not choose those paths (or don't realize they have those choices available) can stagnate and become stuck. Eventually, they can feel hidden "behind the mask." As Shannon L. Adler put it, "One of the greatest regrets in life is being what others would want you to be, rather than being yourself."

Personal choice isn't alone sufficient, but it is necessary, for any kind of meaningful cultural change. People have to be able to decide, on their own, that they want to believe in something and honor it—and there's no getting around this. You can give people every tool, every option, and all the time in the world, but if they don't choose to make something work, nothing will work because that's the choice that's been made. By the same principle, though, you can *remove* every tool, option, and resource from someone who *has* chosen to make something happen, and they just might make it happen anyway. Choice is always a key factor.

There's an observable correlation between choice and work effectiveness. Along a spectrum of performance—weaker at one end, stronger at the other—high performers are almost always people who have *chosen* to perform well in some way. Partly, this should inform who rises fastest, but it should also remind leadership that they have to influence and not merely direct the people following them, in such a way that people are encouraged to choose the best way forward for their work and professional development.

I have two main suggestions for developing a more authentic culture. You can expand upon these in ways sensible to your organization, but for now they should provide two starting points for showing your team what they need to remember about one another in order to open up, to become more honest, and to focus themselves upon the work as a unit.

Reverse Mentoring

Reverse mentoring has been very successful in the tech world—and in their version of reverse mentoring, executives will spend time with teenagers to learn about what's new and popular in technology. The execs get an entirely different perspective this way; they learn more about what's up-and-coming; they can become more aware of their own leadership shortcomings with respect to technology.

It's much the same idea in any field. No matter what kind of company you lead, you can find out how your culture is taking shape by getting word about it from the people at the "bottom." Have your youngest people teach you about their expertise, about their jobs, or even about the company you both work for; you might be surprised when their "version" is different from yours. Culture doesn't always translate perfectly from your intentions to their reality—in fact, it very rarely does!

This requires that the person being reverse-mentored have sincere intentions—that they not be "on a witch hunt" for people who have the "wrong idea." The younger person doing the mentoring has to feel comfortable that there won't be repercussions for what they say or do during that period. Not least of all, leaders need to have a commitment to act upon what they learn, to make good on the learning experience. By opening themselves to this experience, leaders can sometimes get a surprising amount of help with high-level problems even from the entry-level employees in their company.

Some organizations use tools like surveys to gauge how a culture is taking root (or not) within an organization, and you might be able to some of the same good insight from a survey. But surveys rarely get a full response—and on surveys, there's always the possibility that people will write something untruthful because they believe it's what the people reading want to see. If something about a workplace is keeping you from acting authentically, why should it be any different on a survey?

Cracking Implicit Biases

Let's unpack the term *implicit bias* for a moment. A bias is, of course, a prejudice. And something implicit is unspoken—in this case, it's something people may not even realize consciously. In other words: we have to crack implicit biases because they distort our thinking and, in many cases, we don't even realize we have them.

Implicit bias often involves topics like race, gender, and age—and though it can come overtly (as racism, sexism, or ageism), many implicit workplace biases are subtler. For example, it might be expected that employees (male or female) without children are able to work longer hours than those who have children. That's not necessarily fair, but it is a common expectation.

Another subtle implicit bias is the notion—in some companies—that the senior members of a team are the most knowledgeable, or have the final word. It might also be considered customary for new members to "earn their seat" before making serious contributions to any discussion. Think about Maya—we'll come back to her in a moment.

There are two things that are important to observe and remember about these kinds of implicit workplace biases. First: since biases are prejudices—and since prejudices, matter-of-factly, are opinions not based in reason or actual experience—it's distorted and unwise to proceed with knowingly biased thinking. Second: these biases occur at a cultural level, insofar as they are common assumptions, to the point that they often need not (or simply will not) be spoken. These kinds of implicit biases become "how things work around here." Therefore, they are worth the effort to unravel and correct.

Back to Maya. What she could not have known is that she was entering a work culture with implicit biases against her hallmark behaviors—namely, contributing and sharing of her expertise openly, despite her newness at the company. She'd been encouraged to do so because, when she asked about the company's culture, the description given seemed to encourage her to contribute. The company had described the culture one way, and in some ways that description was true in practice—but in other ways, it *wasn't* true in practice, and it's those ways that stifled Maya several weeks into her tenure.

There was more that Maya could have done (especially with extra orientation) to learn about the culture and its origins, soak up its core values and behaviors and communication styles, and to assess the team members she'd call her own as she ripened with the company. But there's more leadership can do to focus on their own companies—consider running a search for implicit bias tests, whether for individuals or for companies in your field.

The System Works, The System Called Reciprocity

All things culture and authenticity, especially in a shared company effort, are two-way streets. Everyone has to respect things the same way, whether that's the values and mission or, most especially, one another.

Many organizations talk about their values, and they hope those will be embodied in the culture they create—but it takes individuals who live those values on a daily basis, who use them to produce the desired outcome. At the end of the day, we all have choices; we can choose to challenge "the box" and maybe free others from their own, or we can stay in the box—or opt out and quit.

Someone once said, "Be the leader you want to work for and the employee you want to work with." When people are free to act authentically, and when cultures encourage people to give genuinely of themselves to the work at hand, they are natural leaders because they represent something greater than themselves.

On this two-way street, the system called reciprocity works. Leaders, give an earnest effort and extend your hand to your employees—and employees, remember that an extended hand helps you up rather than picks you up. People choosing to give and receive, to help one another and serve their work of themselves . . . that's a culture of people, not personalities.

ABOUT THE AUTHOR

April L. Taylor

MBA, PHR

April L. Taylor is an Organization Developer for Humana—an internal consultant role focused on organization design and development across the enterprise. She's an engineer with a big personality—always propelled by a desire to learn and not afraid to do something different.

Though no longer a practicing engineer, April remains a techie with a passion for problem-solving, and she retains many of her foundational skills from engineering. She has been exposed to disciplines spanning aerospace and defense to manufacturing to healthcare—and within functions ranging from HR to management consulting to systems engineering, each one building upon the others. This wide variety of experiences has given April a diverse toolkit for making a real impact.

April is an active mentor for the Kentucky National Black MBA Association chapter's Leaders of Tomorrow program, as well as an active member of the National Society of Black Engineers and Epsilon Gamma Iota, Inc. (a social and service organization), and the National Association of Women MBAs as a board member for the Louisville chapter.

April was recognized as one of the 'People You Should Know' in the winter 2014 edition of *US Black Engineer and Information Technology* magazine.

April is actively coaching and is currently working on her ICF coaching credential.

In her spare time, April enjoys reading, traveling, and volunteering. She has a fur-baby named Sunday.

EMAIL aptaylor3@gmail.com
PHONE 615-554-5672
LINKEDIN /in/apriltaylor3

CPSIA information can be obtained
at www.ICGtesting.com
Printed in the USA
BVHW072224200619
551557BV00002B/239/P